AUDITION ARSENAL FOR WOMEN IN THEIR 30s

101 Monologues by Type,
2 Minutes & Under

AUDITION ARSENAL
FOR WOMEN IN THEIR 30s

101 Monologues by Type,
2 Minutes & Under

EDITED BY JANET B. MILSTEIN

MONOLOGUE AUDITION SERIES

A Smith and Kraus Book

A Smith and Kraus Book
Published by Smith and Kraus, Inc.
177 Lyme Road, Hanover, NH 03755
www.smithandkraus.com

First Edition: August 2005
10 9 8 7 6 5 4 3 2 1

Manufactured in the United States of America
Interior Text Design by Julia Gignoux, Freedom Hill Design
Cover design by Alex Karan of Blaise Graphics, www.blaisegraphics.com

The Library of Congress Cataloging-In-Publication Data
Audition arsenal for women in their 30s ; 101 monologues by type, 2 minutes and under / edited by Janet B. Milstein. —1st ed.
p. cm. — (Monologue audition series)
Includes bibliographical references.
ISBN 1-57525-398-4
1. Monologues. 2. Acting—Auditions. I. Milstein, Janet B. II. Series.

PN2080.A78 2005
812'.045089287—dc22
2005044121

Acknowledgments

I would like to express my deepest gratitude to
Eric Kraus and Marisa Smith for entrusting me with this project
and for their wisdom, patience, and generosity.

I would also like to thank the following people
for their help and support:

Karen Milstein
Barbara Lhota
The Milsteins
Alex Karan
Russ Tutterow
Sandy Shinner
Keith Huff
Karen Vesper
Tom Volo
Julia Gignoux
Susan Moore

All of the wonderful actors who took the time to give their input
and all of the talented writers who shared their work with me.

Contents

INTRODUCTION xi
TIPS FOR SELECTING AND PREPARING A MONOLOGUE xiv

WACKY/QUIRKY/ODD

The Vegan by Keith Tadrowski (comic) 1
Hungover from the 80s by Adrien Royce (comic) 2
Unethical Dilemma from *Occupational Hazards* by Mark McCarthy
    (comic) 3
Asian Invasion by Lauren D. Yee (comic) 5
In Ted's Garage from **Face Value** by Janet Allard (comic) 7
Dog Stories by Keith Huff (comic) 8
Posada by Jeremy Menekseoglu (comic) 9
Bethlehem, PA by Suzanne Bradbeer (comic) 10
A Long Hard Rain by Jason Furlani (comic) 11
The Celery Conspiracy by Merri Biechler (comic) 12

MATERNAL

Away Message by Kelly DuMar (comic) 13
Acceptance Letter by Barbara Lhota and Janet B. Milstein (dramatic) . . 14
Golden Gate by Linda Eisenstein (dramatic) 15
Baby Talk by Jeanne Dorsey (seriocomic) 16
Twin Towers by Ira Brodsky and Barbara Lhota (dramatic) 17
If This Isn't Love by Jonathan Bernstein (seriocomic) 18
Lone Star Grace by Suzanne Bradbeer (dramatic) 19
The Journal by Barbara Lhota and Janet B. Milstein (dramatic) 20
Day Care by Cynthia Franks (dramatic) 21

JOYFUL/ENTHUSIASTIC/EXCITED

Tales from the SaltMines by Mara Lathrop (comic) 23
Lone Star Grace by Suzanne Bradbeer (comic) 24
Lone Star Grace by Suzanne Bradbeer (comic) 25
Cosmic Goofs by Barbara Lindsay (comic) 26
Golden Gate by Linda Eisenstein (seriocomic) 27

Erratica by Reina Hardy (comic) 28
The Slow Convenience by Adam Simon (seriocomic). 29
Thing Quartet by Mark Harvey Levine (seriocomic) 30

BLUNT/DIRECT

Nice Tie from *Romantic Fools* by Rich Orloff (comic) 31
Don't Call Me Loretta by Nancy Gall-Clayton (comic) 32
Epiphany Cake by Kelly Younger (dramatic). 33
The Usual by Barbara Lindsay (seriocomic) 34
Bookends by Jonathan Dorf (comic). 35
Air Traffic by Lauren D. Yee (comic) 36
Hub by Ann Garner (dramatic) 37
Jihad Jones and the Kalashnikov Babes by Yussef El Guindi (comic) . . . 38
Sueño by Scott McMorrow (dramatic). 39

VULNERABLE/HURT/EXPOSED

Among Friends and Clutter by Lindsay Price (dramatic) 40
The Mating Habits of Frogs by Barbara Lhota
    and Ira Brodsky (dramatic) 41
Couldn't Say by Christopher Wall (dramatic) 42
A Bushel of Crabs by Kathleen Warnock (dramatic). 43
Jello Shot by Christopher Wall (dramatic). 44
The Wars of Attrition by Suzanne Bradbeer (seriocomic) 45
Mornings After by Kate Monaghan (dramatic) 46
Lie Down with Dogs by N. M. Brewka (dramatic) 47
Razing the 'Rents by Cynthia Franks (dramatic). 48
Red Light, Green Light by Erik Patterson (dramatic) 49

MELODRAMATIC

The Mandible by Elaine M. Hazzard (comic). 50
Lucy Devil Has Wealth Syndrome by Chris Howlett (seriocomic). 51
Possums by Keith Huff (seriocomic) 52
High Noon by Jo J. Adamson (comic). 53
Rapture by Ruth Tyndall Baker (seriocomic). 54

Mercy Falls by Jeni Mahoney (seriocomic) 55
Fear and Loathing on the Nile by Suzanne Bradbeer (comic) 56
To Mrs. Robinson by Barbara Lhota and Ira Brodsky (comic) 57

ANGRY/FED UP

Last Love by Peter Papadopoulos (seriocomic) 58
Fast Friends by Adrien Royce (dramatic) 60
Hurricane Iris by Justin Warner (seriocomic) 62
Black Flamingos by Julius Galacki (dramatic) 63
The B Side by Katharine Clark Gray (comic) 64
Lonely Girl by Cameron Rabie (dramatic) 65
The Abundance by Paul Heller (dramatic) 66
Erratica by Reina Hardy (comic) 67
While the Baby Sleeps by Aline Lathrop (dramatic) 68
Visions from *The Food Monologues* by Kerri Kochanski (dramatic) . . . 69

PERSUASIVE/INSPIRATIONAL

Queen Bee by Dennis Schebetta (seriocomic) 70
Jersey by Hugh Fitzgerald (seriocomic) 72
An Unfinished Room by Mark Rosenwinkel (seriocomic) 73
Tweaking by Barbara Lhota and Ira Brodsky (comic) 74
Painting by Numbers by Dennis Schebetta (seriocomic) 75
Riot Standard by Katharine Clark Gray (seriocomic) 76
Privates by Janet Allard (comic) 77
Erratica by Reina Hardy (comic) 78

HIGH-STRUNG/NEUROTIC/STRESSED-OUT

"Will You Please Shut Up?" by Dan O'Brien (comic) 79
Hungover from the 80s by Adrien Royce (comic) 80
Avenging Grace by Terri Campion (seriocomic) 81
Dangerous Times by Jean Reynolds (seriocomic) 82
Mercy Falls by Jeni Mahoney (seriocomic) 83
Paintings from *The Van Gogh Exhibit* by Matt Fotis (comic) 84
Meal Ticket by Kit Wainer (comic) 85
Missed Connections by Barbara Lhota and Ira Brodsky (comic) 86
Off Compass by Kelly Younger (seriocomic) 87
Neurotic Splendor by Adrien Royce (comic) 88

LONELY/YEARNING

Almost Full Circle at the Guggenheim by Dianne M. Sposito
(seriocomic) 89
Better Places to Go by David-Matthew Barnes (seriocomic) 90
Romance by Barbara Lhota (seriocomic) 91
Carnality by Mark Loewenstern (dramatic) 92
The Space Between Heartbeats by Kathleen Warnock (dramatic) 93
Baby Talk by Jeanne Dorsey (seriocomic) 94
Erin Go Bragh-less by John Shea (dramatic) 95
Heaven and Home by Matthew A. Everett (seriocomic) 97
The Test by Paul Kahn (dramatic) 98

SEXUAL/FLIRTATIOUS

Brave New Tiger by Diane Lefer (seriocomic) 99
From Zero to Sixty in 3.5 Seconds by Deni Krueger (dramatic) 100
Green-Eyed Monster by Dennis Schebetta (comic) 101
Mutual Mastication by Justin Warner (comic) 102
Hot Tub Haggle by Werner Trieschmann (comic) 103
Phoebe Makes the News by Terri Campion (comic) 104
Stages by Jennifer Kirkeby (comic) 105
Herbert and Marian in the Attic by Matthew J. Hanson (comic) 106
Imagine the Love from _Everyman_ by Elena Kaufman (comic) 107
Elliot (A Soldier's Fugue) by Quiara Alegria Hudes (dramatic) 108

PERMISSIONS 109

Audition Arsenal Introduction

Redefining the monologue book

When Eric Kraus approached me about editing a new series of monologue books based on character type, some questions immediately came to mind: Was this type as in theater or film? Most specific types fall under film, yet monologues are rarely used for film or on-camera. For theater there are really only three main types: Leading Man/Lady, Ingénue/Young Man, and Character Actors. If I wanted to offer more detailed types, what criteria would be most useful? Would profession be considered a type? How about funny? Could social status define type?

In addition, I considered what was needed in a monologue book that had not yet been addressed. How would I improve upon the monologue books I own? What would make a book more valuable? How could I create a book to solve the problems my students are constantly voicing? As an actor, writer, and monologue coach, I wanted this new monologue series to give actors what they truly need for auditions. I had my own ideas about what *I* would find useful, but I decided to poll some actors to get their input, as well. The actors had a lot of common requests that confirmed my initial instincts. Most importantly this series would need to maximize the number of monologues an actor would actually use from one source. To do that, the traditional monologue book would need to be reinvented.

How are the books in this series better?

When I was studying acting in college, I'd always wished that there were monologue books just for actors in their twenties. And my dream books would have taken it a step further and been separated by gender to increase the number of monologues in one book that specifically applied to me. Now, I am presenting that to you — Women 20s, Men 20s, Women 30s, and Men 30s. No more skipping over pages and pages because the characters are out of your age range or not for your gender. Within each book, the choices are plentiful, and you're sure to find pieces that fit your specific needs.

That brings me to the next revolutionary feature of the Audition Arsenal series: The books are organized by type. By type, I'm referring to the most prominent quality the monologue reveals about the actor. So instead of being typed somewhat generically (e.g., waitress or Ingénue), the monologues are designed to show you possess the qualities crucial to a particular character or role. Auditioning for a Harry Kondoleon play? Check out the High-strung/Neurotic/Stressed-Out category. Want to get a callback for that Durang play? Prepare one of the Wacky/Quirky/Odd pieces.

Not only can you use these monologues to audition for a specific role, but you can use them to show your range in general auditions. When asked to prepare two contrasting pieces, you can go beyond simply a comedic and a dramatic (or a contemporary and a classical, if requested), and demonstrate significantly contrasting personas. Put yourself in the director's chair. Which would be more interesting to see an actor perform — a blunt, strong comedic piece with a blunt, strong dramatic piece or a vulnerable comedic piece with an intimidating/dangerous dramatic?

As actors, we must remember that directors are often meeting us for the first time and might assume that we can play only what we show them. So by all means show them! Think of the different impressions you make with your classmates versus coworkers, or on a first date versus a job interview. The pieces you choose tell directors something about you and your capabilities. Sell your strengths, cast yourself against your usual type, and prepare your personal "arsenal" of monologues so you'll be ready for any upcoming audition — no matter what it calls for.

Here are some additional bonuses you'll find in this series:

- The monologues are two minutes and under — some are one minute and under — to fit the time constraints of auditions.

- Very few, if any, of the monologues sound classical. Why? If you are required to do a classical and a contemporary monologue, you want them to contrast as much as possible.

- Only a small number of the monologues require dialects or accents. Why? The rule of thumb is to avoid dialect pieces in auditions unless they are specifically requested. If your accent is not dead-on directors tend to focus on the accent rather than the acting.

- There are 101 monologues to choose from in each book!

- The monologues are from plays as opposed to self-contained pieces. Some of the writers, kindly, at my request, edited the pieces slightly or pasted dialogue so that the monologues would be better suited to audition situations. However, when you read the play, you will see the bulk of the monologue in the same form and that the character and his or her situation have not changed.

- I have included a Tips section in each book containing helpful information that pertains to the selection and preparation of monologues.

I hope you find this new monologue series to be as valuable, time-saving, and innovative as I have set out to make it. In this particular book, I anticipate that you'll find a plethora of monologues to use for upcoming auditions. But don't let that stop you from checking out all of the books in the Audition Arsenal series. I wish you the best of luck in all of your endeavors. And when auditioning, have fun and break a leg!

Janet B. Milstein

Tips for Selecting and Preparing a Monologue

Selection

Choose monologues that make you laugh, cry, feel, or think: "I can relate to this!" If a piece speaks to you, even it makes you angry, chances are you will naturally be invested in the piece.

Although each monologue in this book falls into your age range, you should still consider whether you could realistically be cast in this role. If not, choose another piece.

Find a piece that helps you shine. When reading a monologue ask yourself if it really shows what you can do or if it sells you short.

If you are selecting a monologue for a specific role in an upcoming audition, be sure the monologue reveals that you possess the crucial qualities needed to play that role.

If you are preparing for generals and are selecting two or more monologues, choose contrasting pieces that effectively demonstrate your range.

The monologues in this book are two minutes and under. However, you may have auditions that ask for two monologues to be performed in three minutes, or for one minute monologues. When choosing pieces, make sure they fit the requirements. It is not professional to run over time. In some cases you may even be timed. Therefore, it is best to keep your monologue at least ten seconds shorter than the allotted time slot. Also, keep in mind when you are reading and timing your monologue(s) that performing time will run longer than reading time.

Pick your monologue(s) now! Don't put it off. Choosing a monologue that fits you well, reading the play, and working and memorizing the piece all take time. If you wait until the last minute, you will not be adequately prepared. Unlike cold readings, monologues give you the chance to show what you're capable of when you have time to prepare a piece.

Preparation

In terms of preparing a monologue for use in auditions, there is much work to be done. Depending on where you are in your process and which methods you are studying, you will work differently. However, I find the following steps to be useful regardless of the method you subscribe to and the extent of your acting experience.

Read the play your monologue is from in its entirety. It will help you to understand the character, history, relationship, setting — everything that is needed even when you only perform the monologue. Not only will it help you to clarify your choices and understand the circumstances, but you just might find a new role, play, or author to add to your list of favorites!

If you have difficulty locating the play, look in the permissions section in the back of the book to contact the author or the author's agent to obtain a copy. If that information becomes outdated, check with Smith and Kraus to see if they can help put you in touch with the right person.

Answer the questions below with respect to your monologue and write your answers in the first person (e.g.: I am twenty-eight, I want her to . . .).

Who are you talking to? Make it very specific, not just "a friend" or "Kate." Use the script for clues about your relationship and fill in the rest.

What is your objective (goal, intention, "fighting for")? It must include the other person. What do you want from him/her? Make it specific and bold — go for your dream goal!

When and where is this taking place? Be very specific as it will inform your environment, your body, and much more.

What happened the moment before the monologue begins? What did the other person say or do that compels you to speak the first line (and the rest of your monologue) right now — not two weeks ago, not yesterday, not an hour ago? The moment before is so important. Test it out and fine-tune it until you have chosen something big enough and personal enough to springboard you into the monologue.

Go through the text of your monologue and with a pencil divide the monologue into beats. Look for the major and minor transitions in the text and use your own system to mark them. Do not skip this step or your monologue will likely be on one note.

How are you going to accomplish your objective — achieve your goal? With tactics or actions. These are the things you do to get what you want. When choosing actions or tactics, put them in the form "to verb" the other person. For example: to beg her, to threaten him, to charm her. Go back to your text, think about your objective, and choose an action/tactic for each beat. Test it out, refine it. The text will help you choose. However, be careful not to be so rigid with this process that your monologue loses spontaneity. Over time, you should change your actions if they get stale.

Personalize your monologue. Are there past events, situations, or other characters mentioned in the text? This is one of the most enjoyable parts of the process — let your imagination run wild and fill in the details that are *not* given in the script (but fall under the given circumstances). Be creative and have fun, but don't stop until you create specifics that will live in you fully.

Memorize your monologue inside out and upside down. I recommend memorizing by rote — quickly and without emotion or expression so as not to get stuck in a line reading. The idea is to drill the lines so well that you never have to be *back in your head* thinking about them when you should be *out in front of you* fighting for your objective from the other person.

Work your monologues with a coach, teacher, director, or fellow actor. Auditioning can be intimidating and what we do when performing alone often changes in the presence of others. You cannot be truly focused on achieving your goal if you are trying to direct yourself at the same time. Work with someone who will be supportive yet honest. No matter where we are in our acting careers, we never stop growing and we all need other people to help guide us.

Acting is a shared experience between performers and audience — even when performing monologues. Remember, you may be auditioning by yourself, but you still have an audience and they're rooting for you.

The Vegan
By Keith Tadrowski

Brittany: thirty-seven

Comic

The office of a slaughterhouse in a small Illinois town. Brittany is instructing a new employee on filling out order forms. She speaks quickly.

BRITTANY: You'll like working here. And being the new girl's kinda fun, 'cause all the married guys hit on you. Oh, and when you're done with the form, don't forget to sign your name on the bottom, like so. I like to dot my *I*'s with little hearts. I think it's love karma: You know, that if you put enough hearts out into the world, it'll make that special someone fall in love with you. So far, it hasn't worked, but it doesn't hurt to try, right? To be honest, I haven't had a boyfriend since grade school, but I know the perfect guy's out there. He'll be tall and built and handsome and collect Beanie Babies just like I do. Jeannie O'Reilly in accounting says I'm gonna die alone 'cause I act like a twelve-year-old, but who wants to act like they're thirty-seven? Jeannie also complains I talk too much. Well, I can't help it if I start talkin' about, say, I dunno, Justin Timberlake or the Olsen Twins, and suddenly it's twenty minutes later. Jeannie and me were best friends for a while, but she avoids me now. I guess 'cause she blames me for her nervous breakdown or something. You know, we should hang out some time. Jeannie O'Reilly is a whore. You should come with tonight to my church group, we're doing Christian Karaoke. It's just like regular karaoke, but you sing songs about Jesus. Most of them are just normal songs, but they change a few of the words. My favorite I do is Joan Jett. *(Singing to the tune of "I Love Rock and Roll.")* "I love Jesus Christ! So put another dime in the church box, baby! I love Jesus Christ! So come and take your time and pray with me!" You know, stuff like that. Jesus hates Jeannie O'Reilly. So will you come? People are starting to look at me funny there, and I don't want to have to go again alone. So you'll go, right?

Hungover from the 80s
By Adrien Royce

Rachel: late thirties, a splendid neurotic approaching one of her many midlife crises

Comic

Rachel is applying for a job. She is talking to the president of the company.

RACHEL: Oh, hobbies. I play tennis? Well, I used to. Not so much anymore. I like reading a lot. Well actually I enjoy spiritual books a lot. Well, I'm sort of a Christian. Well, actually my parents are Jewish, but I was always attracted more to churches than temples. It just always seemed like people coming and going from churches were a lot happier than the ones at temples. You know it was the difference between — *(She mimics the dark, tragic Hebrew chanting.)*

Aiughhhhhh!! And —
(She sings.)

"Oh Tidings of Comfort and Joy." And, then I remember laughing hysterically the first time I heard spoken Hebrew at a Jewish wedding. My mother had to take me out into the hall — that was the beginning of the end of my relationship with the Jewish faith. Anyway so I became a born-again Christian when I —
(Frustrated that Mr. Johnson tried to interrupt.)

— when I went through my first midlife crisis. I went through it at thirty. One of my many therapists was a Jesuit priest. So my priest slash therapist said "if you are ever confused with what you want to do just watch what you do every day." At the time, of course I was much too crazy to understand what that meant, but the past couple of months, while I've been taking these interviews with your firm, I think back on that —

— and every day all I think about is getting this job, so you see, it is all as it should be . . .
(She is content with what she just said.)

I consider this job a terrific way to begin the next period of my life. You know I'm a Libra.

Unethical Dilemma
from *Occupational Hazards*
By Mark McCarthy

Arlene: thirties, a cocktail waitress who's seen it all

Comic

Arlene is in her thirties and fed up with her job as a cocktail waitress. On the advice of friends, she's trying her hand at substitute teaching at an elementary school. Old habits are hard to break. A classroom. We may hear the sound of thirty elementary school children misbehaving. Enter Arlene Del Gato. She's late and harried. She tries to get started right away.

ARLENE: Good morning, class, my name is Arlene, and I'll be your waitress this evening. I mean your teacher. And this morning. And I mean Miss Del Gato. Why don't I just start over?
(She leaves the room. She reenters.)
 Good morning class, my name is Miss Del Gato, and I'll be your teacher this morning. Can I start you off with a cocktail?
 Damn it! Damn it, I knew I would screw this up. It was right in that handout that I'm not supposed to say cock. Or screw.
 COCK COCK COCK! SCREW SCREW SCREW!
(She pulls herself back together. She reads a note.)
 So today we're discussing . . . ethics.
(Pause, puzzled.)
 Who can tell me what ethics is?
(Pause.)
 Damn it.
(Pause, desperate.)
 Here's a shiny new quarter for whoever can tell me the definition of ethics.
(Pause.)
 Hardball, eh?
(Pause, wields a cell phone.)
 If I don't have the definition of ethics from someone in the

next five seconds, my boyfriend will kick the living bejesus out of every last one of you, and if I hear one word of protest; ONE WORD, I will slap this whole class with a sexual harassment suit so fast it will make all your stinking little heads spin!

(Pause.)

Really? My God! Thank you.

(Pause.)

This "ethics" can be easily avoided with the careful use of a condom.

Questions?

Asian Invasion
By Lauren D. Yee

Professor Wong: male or female, mid-twenties to late thirties; a severe, crafty-looking Asian American who schemes to take over the world with fellow Asians.

Comic

Professor Wong speaks to a panel of fellow Asian conspirators who have gathered for a secret conference. Professor Wong explains their plans to take over the world — typical stuff from the model minority.

PROFESSOR WONG: Good evening, Ms. Wong. Mr. Wong. Dr. Wong. Miss Wong. Everyone's here. Except for Hong, Song, and Pong. In the future, I think it would be a good idea to find Asian people with last names that don't rhyme. It's no wonder no one takes us seriously. *(Returns to matter at hand.)* Well then, this meeting of the Secret Order of the Brothers Hop Sing is hereby called to order. Today we shall take over the world! Yes, our last plan fell through, what with them picking up Agent Lee. But we've gotten rid of Wen Ho and this time we *will* get the W-88 warhead. Now I know what you're thinking: What are a bunch of Asians supposed to do with a giant nuclear weapon? *(Doesn't know either, thinks.)* Well . . . threaten to blow things up, that's what! *(With growing excitement and fervor throughout the monologue.)* Because no longer will people see Japanese tourists and think they want a picture with Mickey Mouse! No longer will they see a Chinese boy on the street and think he's getting an A in calculus. Instead they will connect us with gangs and thugs and nontraditional family structures! Then we will be able to corrupt America, just like our race has always planned to do! We will reclaim the schools, flood the public education system with thousands of Wongs, Chans, and Lees, and bring back bilingual education so our children will grow up without even knowing their own country's language! *(Getting really worked up.)* Then we'll steal all the menial jobs and insist on getting paid dirt cheap wages for back-breaking labor! Double the hours at half the pay! *(Heaves with anticipation.)* And before baseball games, we'll play Beijing opera! Full volume! And we'll all adopt phony accents so no one will know what the heck we're talking about! *(Laughs maniacally, then after this crescendo, a pause, catches breath, and then, rather quietly with a shrug.)* And if that doesn't work, well . . . we'll just meekly go back to our liquor stores and restaurants and continue infecting the world's food supply with MSG.

In Ted's Garage
from *Face Value*
By Janet Allard

Ted's Mom: thirties, a wacky therapist who professes to be the mother of a young mechanic

Comic

> *When Ted, a young Jiffy Lube mechanic, gets involved with an older woman who wants him to help her with illegal and nefarious activities, Ted's suspicious and over-protective "mom" interrogates him and tries to stop him from leaving her.*

TED'S MOM: How old is this Mrs. McCafferty? What do you know about her, Theodore? What does she want from you? A woman doesn't pick a man up in a Jiffy Lube unless she's really desperate — at the end of her rope — Did she tell you anything strange? Did she look familiar to you in any way? Did she tell you she was your mother, Ted? Did she say that to you? Because crazy women who never had children of their own, when they have the chance, will write letters pretending to be your birth mother and they might even try to find you — Did she tell you she was your birth mother, Ted? Is that who she said she was? You can tell me. Who's always been your mother? I've been your mother. Right Theodore? No matter what anyone tells you, no matter what anyone says, I'M YOUR MOTHER. *(Pause.)* I'm going to have to say, No. Theodore. No, you can't go. N.O. Now, you're going to sit down. In that chair. And take a time out. And we're going to forget these childish dreams about going to India and eating sushi and quitting our jobs and fraternizing with women your own mother's age. We're going to spend some time thinking about common sense. And right and wrong. And our responsibilities to our family and our community. SID-DOWN! Because you are home Theodore. You are with your true love. Your mother. Which is all you ever need. You're with me. And if you move a muscle I'm going to send this car up in blazes like the fourth of July. Do you hear me?

Dog Stories
By Keith Huff

Lucy: twenties to thirties

Comic

Lucy is a cheerful, upbeat, Certified Veterinary Technician whose job it is to inform pet owners that their pets need to be anesthetized. In this scene, to soften the blow, she prefaces the bad news with a dog story of her own.

LUCY: Gary, my husband, is allergic to dogs. After Iris was hit by the Domino Pizza car, Scooter wanted to sleep with us all the time. Like he'd lost his mom, the poor thing. Gary wouldn't hear of it. He sneezes. So I made up the guest room for Scooter. He's got his little bed. His little pillow. His little bird mobile. Before his cataracts made him go blind, he used to lay on his back and stare up at his little birds all the time. Just like a baby, really. Scooter always loved birds. You know how some dogs chase them, bark, that sort of mean-spirited animal-world interaction? Not Scooter. He loved to sit outside, look up into the trees, just watch the birds flit from one branch to the next. I paid a priest a hundred dollars to have him blessed by St. Francis, that's why. We can't do anything about his cataracts, poor thing, because, being diabetic, the doctor doesn't think he'd survive the anesthetic. But after I take him out in the morning for his urine sample, do his blood glucose test, give him his insulin shot, he still likes to sit outside and listen to the birds. The sun coming up, they sing. I can see Scooter's little head turn from one side to the other, listening. Watching him from the kitchen window, I swear he can still see those birds in his own special way. Epileptic, he has his bad days, of course. His first seizure, he went crazy, biting his back leg till it bled. I was warned that things like this usually go all funky with purebred dogs. Gary and I always fight when Scooter has his seizures. Gary wanted to have him put to sleep. I told Gary I'd rather divorce him than do that to Scooter. So he left me.

Posada
By Jeremy Menekseoglu

Beth: twenties to thirties, nurse's assistant

Comic

After all the years of pretending and lies, Beth is finally getting married. And she refuses to let a little thing like the complete mental breakdown of her fiancé, Officer Bruno Posada, spoil the happy occasion. She enters as she always does, in full conversation and oblivious to him staring blankly at the television and thinking of unsolved murders and horror.

BETH: *(Smiles.)* I had the most wonderful day, baby. I went to the-uh-the store, an' I looked at cakes, an' I looked at dresses with my friend Irene. An' I went to work late. An' I din' get in trouble 'cause they got these people now at the hospital that is doin' these tests on the cancer patients.
(Laughs.)

Listen to this, they did some kind of research that cancer smells, right? I don' even know what they're talkin' 'bout 'cause, like, I only been there a month, but they say that it has a smell . . . So . . . Uh, what was I sayin'?

(Lost.) Shit.

(Pause.) Oh yeah, so like they got this — these dogs that smell for like, drugs, an' bombs'n.

(Laughs.) An' they teach 'em to smell out lung cancer and like skin cancer'n shit. So these assholes got this little dog runnin' around the cancer ward, smellin' everythin', and it takes a big ole shit on the floor. An' I'm like, "I ain't cleanin' up after no dog, 'cause it's bad enough I gotta clean up after the cancer people." SO they like, "You better clean up after this here dog, 'cause he's the future of medical research." I'm like, "that dog there? The one lickin' its own ass?"

(Laughs.) They jus' got all mad'n shit.

(Frowns.) You wanna go in the bedroom?

Bethlehem, PA
By Suzanne Bradbeer

Bunny: thirties, a former stripper trying to make a new life in a new town

Comic

> *Bunny has recently left stripping and taken up modern dance instead. She has been practicing her new dance in her handsome new neighbor's backyard and after surprising each other in the dark, she has finally convinced him to take a look at what she's created. Excited, nervous, and wildly attracted to him, she has just taken a swig of Jack Daniels from his flask as she prepares to start her dance.*

BUNNY: OK, so they call this the "Christmas City" right, and this is — ta-da! — a Christmas Pageant dance for the Birth of Jesus. Do you mind if I have another swig? Thanks. *(She drinks from the flask.)* Except, OK, it's kind of radical: It's a sort of fantasia ode-to-*Joseph* 'cause I for one, always thought Joseph gets kind of short shrift with all that Babe-in-a-Manger Broohaha, you know? I mean Joseph, look at him, he's a plain guy, right? I know he's descended from kings or whatever, but he's no philosopher or deep thinker, and here *she* comes — and this is back in the day remember — here she comes saying she's pregnant *by-the-hand-of-God,* and I mean, what would *you* say to that? What would anybody, angel or no angel? But he stood by her. And I just find that so, beautiful. Don't you? Everyone else, it's all Jesus this and Mary that, and I appreciate them, I do, but Joseph, he's the one that really speaks to me in all this. So I'm hoping they will use my tribute to him in part of the festival this year. Tradition or no tradition, there must be room in the Christmas City for a little Joseph — I mean, shake it up people!! *(She waits, seems to be expecting something, suddenly nervous.)* OK, I have one question before I show you. How do you feel about Barry White? Because I just wanted to, if you didn't like Barry, and I hate to sound harsh, but I just wouldn't think you'd have anything to say to me. Not to say that my dance is in any way Barry-y, but, he's kind of my barometer for cultural criticism. *(A deep breath.)* OK, here we go.

A Long Hard Rain
By Jason Furlani

Lola: thirties, a bartender at a local dive bar in upstate New York. A handsome woman from a rural background, Lola is currently studying psychology, which compounded with her experience behind the bar, gives her just enough knowledge to be dangerous.

Comic

> *Lola, having organized a quasi group session of unwilling participants, tries to empathize with Dave, the angriest of the group, who wants to leave.*

LOLA: I can see I have my work cut out for me. But a true healer must be able to work with any circumstance. *(Beat.)* I sense your pain. And I know how hard it is to look that pain square in the eye. See, I had a pet sheep once. Lil' Blue. Had the cutest little "baaa . . ." Soft and cuddly . . . Never pooped on my feet . . . But Lil' Blue did have one flaw. He loved to wander. And when he would wander we would go and find him and we would GRAB him by the ear and shake him and say, "No, no Lil' Blue. Don't wander. There are bad, bad things out there. EVIL THINGS!" So, sure enough, one day Lil' Blue went wandering. And we looked and looked. But by the time we found him . . . the coyotes had got him. Sons-a-bitches didn't leave nothin' but a pile a fluff and his severed Lil' Blue head. And there we were, with our sad little hearts. And we leaned down, and picked Lil' Blue up by his Lil' Blue ear, looked him straight in the one eye them fuckers left, and said, "You see you dumb, stupid jerk! You hadda wander off! Now you're DEAD!" So, see, I know your pain. And I don't want to see another Lil' Blue. Look me in the eye. Don't be a Lil' Blue.

The Celery Conspiracy
By Merri Biechler

Celia: thirties

Comic

> *Celia and Bob have been married twelve years and have three children. On the morning of Celia's mother's funeral, Celia snaps while making the Jell-O mold and tells her sister she's having an affair with the town pharmacist. It doesn't take long for the news to reach Bob. In total disbelief, Bob demands an explanation and Celia confesses.*

CELIA: I lied to you, Bob, I'm not having an affair with the pharmacist. Richard the pharmacist doesn't know me from Eve. The idea came to me this morning while I was making the Jell-O mold and before I knew it, I was saying it out loud like it had really happened, and the more I said it, the better I felt! I know you don't believe me when I say it has nothing to do with you. You're my husband, I love you. I can imagine it's quite a shock to hear your wife is having an affair. But sometimes a girl needs a little excitement and I never meant for it to get out of hand . . . but here you are, all hurt. It's sort of like a few years back . . . when you wanted that bass boat. You believed with all your heart that bass boat was going to give you something you didn't have. This is the same for me. I don't fish. But I do want a little excitement in my life. Aren't you bored with me, Bob? I'm bored sick of me and somehow having an affair with Richard the pharmacist, even if it was only in my head, made me exciting. I did this for us. For our marriage. I never meant for you to hear about it, it was going to be my secret. Because it made me special and you deserve to be with someone special. So that's the truth of it, Bob. The whole truth. I love you. And I'm not having an affair with Richard the pharmacist. Can you please pass the fruit cocktail?

Away Message
By Kelly DuMar

Cin (short for Cindy): about thirty-five, recently divorced single mother of a thirteen-year-old daughter

Comic

> *Recently divorced from her cyber-sex addicted husband, and trying to finish an online exam for her art therapy degree, Cin must share a computer with her teenage daughter, Tick, while dealing with her ex-husband Tripp's intrusive Instant Messaging. Tick presses for simple yes or no answers to her provocative questions, like, "Can I get a belly ring?" But Cin's answers come from her gut. In this monologue, Cin tries to get her defiant and evasive teenage daughter to tell her where she's going after the football game — before she gets there.*

CIN: *Why* do I need to know where you're going? I'm glad you asked! Sit down. *Because* I am your mother. Always have been. Always will be. Unfortunate, for you, possibly. But true, nonetheless. I'm that person in your life, who, beyond everyone else, and beyond reason or limit, *cares* about where you are going. I care, because it is in my blood and bones to care. I care because, whether or not you're satisfied with the result, I brought you kicking and screaming into this world. And, because I care, more than any other human being has or will ever care about you while you are traipsing over this earth, I need to know where you *are*. Because, if you went missing, by choice or by force, however small that horrible possibility may be, *I* would be compelled to *find* you. If I had to lose my job, become homeless and, snowshoe across Siberia in a blizzard, I wouldn't stop searching until I *had* found you. Now, you may decide, much later in life, when you can no longer afford to avoid therapy, whether this kind of caring is loving devotion or bizarre fanaticism. But, like it or not, I'm on your trail. For life. So, I just need to know where you're going, after the game. Before you get there.

Acceptance Letter
By Barbara Lhota and Janet B. Milstein

Tina: thirty-eight years old, Charlie's mother, works in a bowling alley

Dramatic

> *Tina, thirty-eight years old, Charlie's mother, hides his acceptance letter to a prestigious school out east. He's furious and hurt when he discovers this betrayal. Tina, heartbroken by the idea of him leaving their small town in Michigan to go off to Boston, defends their hometown and pleads with him to put off college for just one more year.*

TINA: It's not a nothing town! It may not be as intellectual or cultured as you'd like, but there are nice people here. They're good people, and they have been very, very good to us. I had nothing but a bunch of bruises and a shattered ego when I arrived here. I got a job, and I made good friends and I built a bowling league at the bowling alley that's alive, and active. It's a good . . . it's a nice life. You could just stay one more year. Go to school at Alpena Community College. Just a year. Just a year. It's not that bad. I'll work part-time at Walgreen's to make extra cash. Then you'll go away next year, and you won't have to take out as much in student loans. Meanwhile you enjoy the lake and water skiing. You work at the forest preserves for extra cash. We'll throw three major kick-butt cookouts a summer. I don't have small expectations for you, Charlie. I know you're special. I've always known. Don't you get it? *(Beat.)* I don't want you to leave.

Golden Gate
By Linda Eisenstein

Evelyn: thirties, too fast and too loud

Dramatic

> *A broke, manic Evelyn has impulsively decided to move to California with her teenage son Jake, who is an irresistible force against the idea. Jake believes that it's a lame ploy for her to follow her boyfriend Peter across the country. She tries to justify it to Jake.*

EVELYN: *(To her son.)* I'm doing this for you! I am. Jake, you're two years from graduating. And you want to go to college. Well, it isn't going to happen. I can't afford to send you to college here. Your dad sure isn't going to cough it up, not now, not with the new wife. I'm lucky I still get the child support check. In California college is free. Or it used to be. Before Reagan. Anyway, it's still pretty cheap, if you graduate from a California high school. So, see, this is for you. Honest. All we have to do is get you enrolled, and . . . This isn't about Peter, this is about you, this is about your college . . . I'm not, chasing him, it's about your future, Jakey, I want you to make it, somewhere nice, you deserve someplace nice, someplace warm, *(Starting to cry.)* someplace . . . warm.

Baby Talk
By Jeanne Dorsey

Kristin: thirties, single, middle-class, adoptive urban mother

Seriocomic

> *Kristin is sitting on a bench at a playground with two women whose acquaintance she has just made. As her adopted infant Arturo snoozes in his stroller, she explains how she came to be a single adoptive mom.*

KRISTIN: It's never how we imagine it to be. I thought I was straight until I went to discuss a grade with my biology professor and she kissed me hard on the mouth and we ended up living together until graduation. Then she promptly dumped me for a sophomore and of course I thought I'd be alone for the rest of my life. But I ended up having a series of really interesting, exciting, difficult lovers. The last one was Janine and I thought we'd be together forever. Everything seemed to click. We started to talk about kids. We did a lot of reading on alternative lifestyle parenting, you know, artificial insemination, but I wasn't particularly eager to go down that road. So for awhile I assumed we'd go through life together childless. Nobody was talking about adoption for same sex couples but then all of a sudden international adoption makes it all a possibility and the idea stuck. I mean it really stuck as though I'd conceived. It wasn't just in my head, it was in my belly. And Janine got jealous. It was so bizarre. She was jealous of an idea, she thought I was paying more attention to it than to her and I couldn't really disagree with her so she left. That was hard, that was really hard. And it was confusing because I remember thinking, this was before I'd even made arrangements to go to Ecuador to meet my child, I remember thinking "I'm a single parent! I haven't met my child, and don't know its sex but I've become a parent and now I'm a single parent." Before I knew it I was on my way to South America and here I am with Arturo and everything makes sense. I never would have predicted any of what occurred and honestly my life is much more interesting than I'd ever imagined it. I'm definitely not bored.

Twin Towers
By Ira Brodsky and Barbara Lhota

Rose: thirties, serious, lonely, intense

Dramatic

> *Rose is a single woman who adopted a child from Russia. While her best friend Janice admires her dedication as a mother, she fears that Rose is neglecting herself, and that ultimately this is not good for the child. This is Rose's response.*

ROSE: No, you're right. I haven't gone anywhere without her, and she's only four, and I missed the first year of her life. I'll never have those days back. They're lost to me. And I don't want to have any more of those empty places. I'm like a living photo album, and I have tens of thousands of those blank plastic pages to fill, and every minute of every day I fill those pages with Lola. I know that it can't go on forever. I know that she has to grow up and go to play dates without me and day care will become kindergarten will become school and high school, and all those things that children do. So I'm not totally delusional. I know that I'm excessive, and I try to do what I can to keep it from getting out of hand. But I want to gather as many of those moments as I can. And when Lola is older and if she asks me, I can give them all back to her.

If This Isn't Love
By Jonathan Bernstein

Marion: thirty-seven, a wife, mother and part-time paralegal

Seriocomic

Marion sits on a park bench at a playground watching her son roughhouse. She strikes up a conversation with another mother.

MARION: That's yours?
. . . Hm, she's sweet. I've seen you here before with her, you're — it's always nice watching you — very calm — you have a nice way with her, I'm completely completely jealous. Which is not to say that my son doesn't love *me* but it's somehow more complic — excuse me — Jeremy! Jeremy, hey! That's *his* sweater vest! Jeremy!! I just saw you! Give it back! Back!!! Play nice! Thank you!
Ugh. Sometimes . . . I don't know how you do it because I know he's my son but sometimes . . .
Do you work?
. . . . Ah. Great. No, *I* do, a little, I'm only part-time, though, I couldn't give it up entirely, that would drive me totally around the ben — but I'm only part-time, I'm down to fifteen hours a week. His father takes some time off but I'm with Jeremy almost all the time. I'm almost always with him. And — I can hear myself — it's just it's hard, you know, sometimes, just to know what the right thing is these days, that's all. What's acceptable. Spend too much time at home, and you lack ambition; too much time away from home, and you're a monster.
Wouldn't it be nice if Pamela Anderson wrestled Gloria Steinem? In a big pit, really have it out, once and for all. And throw in Hilary Clinton and Donna Reed and Oprah Winfrey and *Bill* Clinton and give them all a big Camille Paglia book to clobber each other with and see who's left standing at the end. Wouldn't that be nice? That would be gratifying. My money's on Oprah. Oprah's tough.

Lone Star Grace
By Suzanne Bradbeer

Barbie Ann DeMarco Sanchez: late twenties to thirties

Dramatic

> *Barbie Ann is a lingerie (foundations) saleswoman who wants to start her life over in Houston. Here she laments the loss of her only baby. She is speaking to her estranged sister.*

BARBIE ANN: I was thinking we'd move to Houston, the two of us, after she was born. We'd move to Houston and start a new life together and I'd work selling Foundations somewhere — I'm really good at that. But she was born too soon — she wasn't even three pounds. Oh my God, she was so little . . . I had thought when she came out that they'd put her on my belly like they do, and I'd feel her all warm and gushy and squirming with life. And she would feel my body so it wasn't such a shock to her coming out into the wide, wide world. But they took her away. Put her in a machine. I saw her before I left the hospital and then I didn't go back again until yesterday. I don't know how I did that . . . I stayed out 'till the crack o' dawn every night and got up to sell underwear every day and somehow I managed not to think about her tiny little hands, her little face, her little . . . Oh God. I was at the hospital all yesterday. It was the first time I saw her since she was born. They called me and told me she was bad off. She'd gotten pneumonia. So I went, I finally went, and she was lying there alone, Annette, surrounded by all this paraphernalia — but she couldn't breathe, she was gasping for breath . . . My baby couldn't get enough breath . . . She saw me though, I think she saw me. I looked into her eyes. Can they see when they're that little? I forgot to ask. I meant to ask that . . .

The Journal
By Barbara Lhota and Janet B. Milstein

Anne: late thirties, Tad's mother

Dramatic

Anne, late thirties, tells a young high school journalism teacher to stop coming on to her gay son because he is far too old for him.

ANNE: Look, I've lived this, OK! Don't give me the bull. Tad's father was five years older than me when I was in high school. He told me we should slow things down too and then we'd pick things up after I graduated. Sound familiar? He'd marry me — he said. I could have the baby and then he'd put me through school. Sounds good on paper. He kept me hanging on to him. Meanwhile, I didn't make friends my own age or plan to go away to college. Every night I came home to talk to him on the phone, and make sure I went to bed early for the baby. When I did graduate, I had to take classes at the community college while I had a toddler in tow. And Tad's father . . . well, he couldn't marry me or put me through college because things had changed. He wanted to go to Europe for grad school. And he had fallen in love with someone else. I don't regret having Tad for one minute — he's the joy of my life, but I do regret not having my youth! And I will not let you strip my son of his senior year and his life to come! He is too young, and you are too old! It is simple as that!

Day Care
By Cynthia Franks

Lori: mid-thirties, long hair

Dramatic

> *Lori has just come into work very late, again. The boss told her last time if she's late one more time, she's fired. She is speaking to Cori who has constantly covered for her since she had her baby. They are graphic designers in the auto industry and share a cubical. Lori enters with a coffee and a bagel as a peace offering for Cori who she knows will be angry with her for being late. They have a big project due; the launch of a new car model at the Detroit International Auto Show in two weeks.*

LORI: I got you a bagel and your favorite coffee; vanilla hazelnut, no sugar. For covering for me. Every day. We'll get it all done. Don't worry. *(Pause.)* Guess what Bradley John did this morning? We were getting ready for daycare and he blew a bubble. It was the cutest thing. The bubble peeked out of his mouth and glinted with light. I didn't know what it was at first. I said to myself, what is that thing glinting in Bradley John's mouth? I saw something like that once before when I was in the hospital when I had Bradley John. It was a plastic cover. I freaked out because I thought he was going to choke. You have to be very careful with infants. So when I saw the same thing in his mouth. That little glint, my heart stopped. But just as I was going to stick my finger in I saw it was a bubble. I don't know why I panicked. I don't even keep a trash can in the baby's room so I don't know why I would think it was plastic. But you never know. I think I was born to be a mother. I could see myself in the bubble. I said, "Oh, Mommy can see herself," and he held on to it, so, I pretended to fix my hair in the bubble and when I was done he popped it and giggled. Then I had to leave to come to work. I feel like I miss whole big chunks of his life that I'll never get back. All those precious moments wasted on strangers at day-care. *(Beat.)*

Gas? You think it's gas? Poor, Bradley John, how could I leave him at day care when he has gas. I'm a terrible mother. Cover for — I don't care. I have to go to my baby.

Tales from the SaltMines
By Mara Lathrop

Pepper: thirties, an overly gung-ho Human Resources professional. She is the epitome of a team player, only with no clue as to the game.

Comic

Pepper, a gung-ho Human Resources Specialist, aspires to be the Friendly Face of a nameless, faceless multinational corporation. In this scene, she does her Rah-Rah HR thing for Martha, the brand-new temporary secretary.

PEPPER: On behalf of the over twenty-seven thousand employees worldwide, it is my distinct privilege, not to mention a real personal pleasure, to present this card-key. In addition to giving you unlimited access to the building between the hours of eight A.M. and six P.M., Monday through Friday except for Thanksgiving, Christmas, New Year's Day and the Fourth of July, this card-key is a symbol of our mutual interdependence with the Company. Wear it always with pride. Actually, you have to keep it prominently displayed on your person at all times for security purposes. A lot of the girls wear them on these wrist scrunchies — the alligator clips can be vicious on polyester, but, gee, that blouse looks almost like it's linen, and, ahhhhh, you're actually going to want to stay away from natural fibers, Martha. Something about the insulation in the ceiling, I don't really know myself. But I'll get you all the memo alerts about fiber conflicts from building maintenance. But, hey, one day — you should be OK for one measly day. Anyway, polyester, nylon, Dacron, rayon, New-Age blends, anything based on fossil fuels, they're all fine, and you can wear your cottons and wools after hours and on the weekends, but do not, I mean DO NOT wear silk. Ever. Oh, and if you see a fine, gray dust on your skin, wipe it off with a dry rag and try to stay away from water for a couple of days. So! Do you like us yet? Finding everything you need? Sliding into good old-fashioned first-day overwhelm?

Lone Star Grace
By Suzanne Bradbeer

Annette Leland Pierce: thirties

Comic

> *Annette is a social-climbing member of a small-town Junior
> League. She has just met a bona fide descendant of a Texas
> hero.*

ANNETTE: Colonel James Walker Fannin? You are a descendant?
What an honor, this is truly an honor. Colonel Fannin and his
men were slain not very far from here — slain, massacred,
butchered in the most vile, bloodthirsty way — what a pleasure
to meet you! I am a member of the Junior League in the City of
Victoria and I would love to have you speak to our group about
your uncle. You'd be in fine company, we've had some very illu-
minating speakers. You'd give a little lecture of some kind, an
inspiring lecture about your uncle and his brave men and you
could bring in how it has affected your life and all our lives for
that matter, because it certainly has — and maybe you could
include a little domestic interest too, like what the wives were
doing and how brave they were and how they went on to inspire
others after their husbands' brutal deaths, and if you know what
kind of meals they cooked for their husbands or if they had ser-
vants to do that and you know, how that compared to the food
on the battlefield — Of course I'd be glad to advise you on what
we'd find interesting, and OH! OH! If you have one or two
recipes that have been passed down through your family then
that would just ice the cake. We do this sweet little cookbook —
for charity you know, and it has all kinds of local recipes in it
including a very good one of mine for Zippy Mexicali Dip. But
that's neither here nor there. Anyway it'd be quite a feather in
my cap to include a favorite family recipe from a bona fide Texas
hero, I'd be so proud.

Lone Star Grace
By Suzanne Bradbeer

Barbie Ann DeMarco Sanchez: late twenties to thirties

Comic

> *Barbie Ann has stopped in a small Texas diner on her way*
> *to Houston. She is very excited about her new life and she*
> *confides this to her new friend, the waitress Persephone.*

BARBIE ANN: Let me tell you something Persephone, this is no fly-by-night-lolly-day excursion, I Have Got A Job! Tomorrow morning when the doors open at the Macy's Department Store in the Galleria of the great city of Houston, *I* will be there. I will be in the Lingerie Boutique ready to help, ready to advise, ready to shower my expertise and Bra School Training on any and all ladies looking to buy Foundations and other Intimate Apparel. And if you don't mind my saying, you possess a very charming bosom there that I could help you accentuate to its full advantage. It's charming, believe me. Anyway — I thought I'd look up Tammy Jo Byerly — in Houston I mean — she was my best friend from the fifth grade and I was so broken-hearted when she moved. I even tried to stow away in their station wagon, but my sister talked me out of it . . . Anyway, it'd be fun to see her — Tammy Jo that is — seeing as she sent me a Christmas card! And she's got that darling brother who used to have a crush on me, not that I'm expecting anything to come of that but he lives in Houston too I think. *(Beat.)*
> So do you think I'm pretty?

Cosmic Goofs
By Barbara Lindsay

She: thirties, is a very emotional woman, spirited and vulnerable and brave, not quite fully recovered from a major heartache.

She is at home alone, which is not unusual for her. She lies on the couch watching TV, expecting nothing special. Then there is a knock on the door.

SHE: Who is it? *(No answer.)* Who is it? *(No answer.)* Hello? *(No answer. She goes to the door and looks through the peephole, then gasps. She races to the mirror and starts fixing her hair.)* I'm coming! *(To the audience.)* Oh my God, oh my God. It's him. You know. The big one. Oh my God, oh my God, I can't believe he's here. I haven't seen him or heard from him since he left. Nobody has ever hurt me that much. A few have tried, of course, but nobody ever even came close. Look at me. I see him one second and all my pores are opening. Oh God, please make him knock again. *(There is a knock on the door.)* Do you see what I mean? The man can read my mind. Very intense connection. He found places in me I didn't even know I had and stirred them up and sent them swooping out into the sky to dance with the angels. I'm not kidding. With him, I suddenly have poetry pouring out of me, and I want to give money to everybody and not eat meat. When I'm with him, my singing sounds like celery growing in a monastery garden, and I'm a terrible singer, I'm telling you. The man can lick my stomach. I am not kidding about any of this. *(She paces in an agony of confusion.)* We never married. He wouldn't. Last I heard, he was not married to my former best friend Colleen and they were living together in the desert. That hurt, losing them both. I hate them. I hate them both very intensely. I thought he'd get bored with her and come back. That was seven years ago. And now he's out there right now, and I can promise you this. He's not going to knock again because he's so sure I'm going to open the door. *(There is a knock on the door.)* Oh my God. He's changed.

Golden Gate
By Linda Eisenstein

Evelyn: thirties, too fast and too loud

Seriocomic

A broke, manic Evelyn has impulsively decided to move to California with her teenage son Jake, who is an irresistible force against the idea. She tries to jolly him into cooperating.

EVELYN: *(To her son.)* OK, Jakey, here's the plan, what a plan, it's a great plan. Hey? We're just going to drop everything — Hah-hah! — and get in the car. And we're going to travel . . . West! *(Sings.)* "California, here we come" — ba-da-da — "right back where I started from!" — ba-da-da — God, Jakey, it'll be great, huh! You're going to love California, baby. I can't believe in all these years I've never taken you there. We'll take Grampa's car. Hell, I drive it more than he does. All we have to do is ask. Well, all *you* have to do is ask. What the hell does he need that car for anyway, he never goes anywhere except to the drugstore for Milk of Magnesia, for that he can use Mom's car. It doesn't make sense, the two of them staring at the TV all day, two perfectly good cars in their garage and us having none. So we'll take his. Atlas, atlas, where the hell did I put my road atlas, Jake, don't sit on your ass, help me find it. *(Picks up a pair of sunglasses and puts them on, pretending to be discovered.)* "How do I look, dahling?" Click-click-click-click. "I know you can't believe you discovered me in that soda fountain, standing next to the soda jerk, God wasn't he a jerk, but that period of my life thank God is over and now I, we, my fabulous son Jake and I, we are . . ." Of course you're going!

Erratica
By Reina Hardy

Lisa Milkmin: thirties, a publicist. She makes an especial point of smiling after each sentence she speaks.

Comic

> *Professor Samantha Stafford has just completed her scholarly book on Shakespeare. Publicist Lisa Milkmin wants to punch it up for the market, but her client is less than friendly. In fact, the two women hate each other. Here, Lisa lays out her plans.*

LISA: Hello, Samantha! Sorry I'm late. I keep telling you, you can call me Lisa. We're all friends here. I brought lattes! You look nice today, nice and clean. No time for gossip, I'm afraid. Things are really starting to happen for us, very new, very exciting. Nice of course, but that means deadlines, doesn't it? Down to brass tacks! Did you read my memo? OK! Well, I'll just have to tell you, then. First, the good news. Plekker and Pannin is really starting to see in you what I see in you, which is potential. Real potential. To bring literature back to the forefront of what people read. P and P think, with the right jacket photo, you could have the biggest success for criticism since *The Invention of the Human.* I read your manuscript for the first five chapters, and it was really stunning. Knocked me over in my seat, let me tell you. But there are a few things I think it's missing. First of all, really, for someone talking about Shakespeare — it is a bit . . . cynical. We're really used to something more life-affirming, warm, you know, the perfect demonstration of essential human truths: love, honor, friendship, love. That goes over well and it makes people feel good. You haven't got that. But I think that's good! That's a . . . selling point. You're edgy, you've got attitude, you're saying something different. And you've got lots and lots of sex. That's sexy, that sells.

The Slow Convenience
By Adam Simon

Ainslie: thirty, a social worker with a slowly eroding conscience and
a never-ending supply of energy.

Seriocomic

> *On Ainslie's thirtieth birthday, someone makes the mistake*
> *of making a joke about getting old; someone else has made*
> *the mistake of feeding her energy drinks.*

AINSLIE: *(Very quickly.)* I don't know what people are talking about
when they say things like that — I mean people who say all that
stuff about turning thirty are always the same people who start
dreading it when they're twenty-four and what's the point of
that? I mean really. I spent my twenties going as fast as I could
and just crashing into things, I felt like I was always one step
away from a collision, but I think my thirties are going to be
totally different. I mean life gets easier right? You figure stuff
out, you move on, you figure the next thing out, and when you
turn thirty something just, POOF, flashes and there it is and you
can't deny it because there it is — I don't see why other people
don't get this. It's like it's a secret and nobody tells anybody
younger because it's our little secret — Danielle, if anyone asks I
didn't tell you, OK, you turn thirty soon anyway, right? — Are
you guys sure there's vodka in this, cause all I taste is the Red
Bull, which is fine, but I ordered — . . . What?. . . I'm not talking fast. I don't know what you're talking about. I think you're
just listening slowly.

Thing Quartet
By Mark Harvey Levine

Becca: thirties, excited and bubbly

Seriocomic

Becca is pregnant, and she has just found out that the baby is going to be a girl. She's speaking to one of her female friends

BECCA: This kid! This girl. Oh my GOD! This girl is driving me crazy! And she's not even born yet! All these . . . things have been arriving. Presents. Spoons. Bibs. Blankets. Toys. Diapers. Bottles. Socks. Bowls. Things! What am I going to do with all these things?! And I still don't even believe I'm going to be a mother. It's all an elaborate hoax. To get people to go to Toys R Us and buy us things. Don't get me wrong. I'm very happy about it. We're both very happy. Happyhappyhappy! And a little stunned. Worried. When the doctor told me it was a girl, I got lightheaded and saw stars! It's like I saw her whole life pass before my eyes. I saw her grow up! And she was a nice person. Very smart! A very smart girl! Played the viola. My mother says the same thing happened when she found out she was having me. Of course, we have a talent for hysterics in my family. Handed down from one hysterical woman to the next. They tease me about it at work. They jump out from around corners just to hear me scream. It's really not nice. But I mean, I want this girl to be . . . I don't know . . . Smart. Funny. Special. And I shouldn't feel guilty for wanting my daughter to be . . . I don't know . . . I want her to be happy, sure, but — a thousand other things, too. But mostly — a smart girl. A smart girl. The thing is . . . Smart girls usually aren't happy.

Nice Tie
from *Romantic Fools*
By Rich Orloff

Woman: thirties to forties

Comic

In a bar, a man has just asked a woman if he can buy her a drink.

WOMAN: Can you buy me a drink, you ask. Oh, I don't know. First you buy me a drink, and then you ask for my phone number, and I figure what the hell, so I give it to you. If you don't call me, I'm disappointed. If you do call me, we go out, and either I don't like you, or I like you and you don't like me. And I'm disappointed. Or we do like each other, and we go out some more, and things become pretty wonderful — great sex, revealing conversations, compatible neuroses — but I discover I want more than you can give. And I'm disappointed.

Or we stay with it, and we get closer and closer and more dependent on each other, which gives us the strength to go through periods of mutual doubts, and things said in anger that we'll pretend to forget but which will come up again during the post-natal depression I'll have after the birth of our first child. *If* we get married, that is, and Lord knows how many friends I'll lose because they like me but they're just not comfortable around you.

After our second child, the unresolved conflicts we buried for the sake of our marriage will propel you into a torrid affair, either with someone you work with or, God forbid, one of my few friends who *is* comfortable around you. I'll try to forgive you, eventually, by which point both our children will be in intensive therapy.

The divorce will be ugly, expensive, and I'll never be able to trust men again, those who aren't frightened off by my sagging features and two sadomasochistic children. The kids'll blame me, of course, and I'll die all alone . . . I think I'll pass on the drink.

Don't Call Me Loretta
By Nancy Gall-Clayton

Loretta: thirties, gritty, sure of herself

Comic

It's almost quitting time, and the waitress in a small, aging diner is less than pleased to see a truck driver come in, no doubt expecting a meal, if not some friendly banter. Before he can order or flirt or get comfortable, Loretta tells him how things are and how they're going to be.

LORETTA: If I were you, I wouldn't get too comfortable, and I wouldn't take too much time reading that menu neither. We don't have half that stuff — ever, and we sure don't have it now. We're closing in five, Mister. Five. I'm the last one here, and I don't linger for nobody. If the president himself walked in here right now, I'd tell him to leave. That's right. When it's five till nine, it's five till nine. Get it? I'm focusing on the nine.

The only thing I will happily sell you right now is a cup of coffee. If that's what you want, fine, just say so, and don't act like this here's the Holiday Inn. The coffee's going on two hours old, and it'll cost you one dollar plus whatever you tip me for taking care of you when it's five minutes till closing. Which should be at least 50 cents, if you want my opinion. Anything less than 50 would be an insult, and you wouldn't want to insult me, now, would you? A dollar would be nice. There's no law against the tip being the same as the bill, you know. You could even tip bigger than the bill. I seen it happen once. But not to me.

Now, if you're really starving and you can't get by on just a cup of coffee, I guess I could give you a pickle. We keep them in brine, and all I have to do is fish one out for you. They cost a dollar, too. Other than that, everything's put up. So, one black coffee and a dill pickle — that's what I'm offering. That's all I'm offering. What'll it be, Mister?

Epiphany Cake
By Kelly Younger

Alice: thirties, African-American, very "New York"

Dramatic

Alice is a novelist sent by her agent to a reading group in suburban Los Angeles. She discovers that no one in the all - white, all-female book group has even read her novel about a slave girl named Daphne making her way to America. After Alice confronts the group for lying, she is forced to reveal that she herself had to lie in order to write a bestseller.

ALICE: Mainstream America is white. And if you want a best-seller, you better write to a white audience. And white America doesn't want to read a story about some black girl dating their white son, and some black girl coming to dine at the country club, and some black girl making something of herself on her own. If it's that kind of story, America needs some distance. Set it a hundred years ago, they said. Make Daphne a slave, they said. Write about the Middle Passage, and plantations, and the civil war, Mr. Lincoln and oh yes, throw in the occasional "yes massah, yes massah" and the readers will eat it up. You'll get every book club stamp from *Oprah* to the *Today Show* and then some. Housewives all across the nation will discuss your book over wine and cheese, or in your case, cake. And who cares if they get it or not, they bought it, and that's money in our pockets. America doesn't care why the caged bird sings or what color purple is. All they care about is relieving their guilt over the past. And my oh my isn't it easier to read a book about black people than to actually talk to some?

The Usual
By Barbara Lindsay

Staci: thirties, is a professional waitress, a no-nonsense woman with
no illusions and no regrets.

Seriocomic

*Staci is fed up with being asked for special treatment by
Clark Kanetta, one of her regular customers. He has
confided that he has just come from the hospital after receiv-
ing bad news.*

STACI: I've got news for you, Clark. You are not special. You're not
special because you have money, you're not special because you
look like every girl's dream, you're not special because you drive
a little fast black car, and you're not special because you're
dying. In fact, not only are you not special, you've got an ego
that runs ahead of you barking like a sled dog team, which in my
opinion makes you more ordinary than most. Just a minute, I'm
not done. So you want me to care? Fine, you come in here and
announce that you are *not* going to die, and I will sit up and take
notice, but until that time you are nothing to me but a guy who
orders me around, can't remember my name, and stiffs me on
tips. Look at me. Look at me good and hard. Look at that
woman with all the extra hair and that little red-headed boy
with the stripy shirt. You think our clocks aren't ticking? You
think our alarms aren't going to go off sometime? Word is out,
Clark. Everybody dies. But with you it's special. With you it's
different. With you it's the only time it ever happened. Because
you're not just anybody, you're Clark Kanetta, man with briefcase, man with car, man with money. Well, the joke's on
you, Mister Get-Me-A-Baked-Potato-And-Get-It-Now, because
you're just as temporary as the rest of us nobodies.

Bookends
By Jonathan Dorf

Susan: an English professor in her mid-thirties, something of a shark

Comic

> *Susan, a predatory English professor in her mid-thirties,*
> *delivers a lecture to her Shakespeare class. Eric, a college*
> *freshman, gets her attention by coming in late — it's the*
> *start of what later turns into an affair.*

SUSAN: Good morning. I am Professor Susan Harris, and the name of this course *(Eric, looking like he's overslept, enters. Susan pauses to watch him.)* is Shakespeare. It should be called Shakespeare's plays, because we don't study his poetry. I don't like all that sissy sonnet crap. Shakespeare, ladies and gentlemen, is about winners and losers. And whatever happens is always the loser's fault. Richard II, consummate loser. Loses his kingdom because he's too slow and pathetic to do anything. It's his fault. Think about it. Why do we care about Richard? It's ludicrous. In fact, I would propose that Richard is actually the usurper and that Henry Bullingbrook was king all along. Richard is therefore filler, and since there are already two plays named after Henry IV, *Richard II* should be eliminated entirely. However, the department is strongly against eliminating *Richard II* from the syllabus, so as a compromise we will be reading only Henry's lines. *(Beat.)*
　　Give me a loser, ladies and gentlemen, and I will give you a place to lay the blame. Did Richard III cry? Of course not. But all those cowardly dukes and princes who committed suicide and tried to frame him did. Richard III met his death the way he met life. With confidence. He went out a winner. Study his speeches with care. Memorize them. You will be tested on them. You will not be asked to remember the losers. You may discard them in literature as you should in life.

Air Traffic
By Lauren D. Yee

Caroline: mid-twenties to early thirties. An uptight, anal-retentive woman who simply enjoys having her way. She isn't a lawyer, but she works at a law firm.

Comic

> *Caroline is on the plane, and Dan has taken her window seat, suspiciously clutching his briefcase. She will stop at nothing to get her seat back.*

CAROLINE: We have two options. I'd consider them carefully, if I were you. Of course I'm not you, which is a fortunate thing. But then we'd have a problem on our hands. And I say "we" because this really is a problem between the two of us. I don't think it's necessary to get the authorities involved and I'm sure you wouldn't want that, would you? So you can either remain where you are, in which case I would have to call the flight attendant and have him or her remove you. But then perhaps I notice that you've been acting oddly and there's something peculiar about your suitcase. You really are much too protective of it for it to be anywhere near normal. And I'm a lawyer, you know. I know the law. And perhaps as you refuse to move, I could suggest to the flight attendant that there's something peculiar with this man's briefcase and hopefully you haven't been stupid enough to go around *hiding* something illegal in there, but I make no claims as to your level of intelligence and so you may very well be hiding huge chunks of uranium in there, not only a huge health hazard but illegal enough to ground the plane, get you kicked off, and send you over to airport authorities. And even if you don't have anything in that briefcase, will it really be evident until this plane is far, far away from you? So either you can let that happen, or you can get out of my goddamn seat so that I can sit down very comfortably and watch us take off from the runway. *(As Dan relinquishes his seat.)* Thank you. *(Adds, pertly.)* I like window seats.

Hub
By Ann Garner

Roo: early thirties

Dramatic

> *Roo and Drew were deeply connected friends who became lovers. But Drew broke it off via e-mail and they have stopped speaking. Now they meet by chance in an airport. Drew is with his secretary/fiancée (the woman he left Roo for). He has just revealed that the girlfriend is pregnant. Roo was deeply hurt by the breakup and seeing Drew again has renewed the wounds for her. Here, working from a place of blind hurt, she tells him some harsh truths.*

ROO: Drew. Or Andy, or Andrew. Whatever you want to call yourself. You're pathetic. This is exactly the kind of thing you were always on your guard about. And you fell for it. She knew she'd never see a ring unless you *had* to marry her. So how'd it happen? No let me guess! All of a sudden, one day, her birth control pill stopped working. She doesn't know how it happened! And this was, let's see, not long after you two had had some terrible fight in which you intimated that you would be better off if you parted. Then this miracle of life happened! Is that about right? Don't bother to deny it. I warned you about her years ago, didn't I? I said she was underhanded, amoral even. The way she pursued you even though you were already with me? I could have told you this would happen. I did tell you this would happen. When did you stop believing me? *(Pause.)* Four months along and not even showing yet? Huh. I bet . . . I bet if you left her, this "baby" would mysteriously disappear into thin air. Fine, tell yourself what you need to. I can't care anymore. And I did care once, so very much. *(Pause.)* I would say I hope you're happy. That would be a generous thing for me to do. But I'm not that generous. And I'm not that good a liar. So I'll just say. Your life could have been extraordinary but you're such a coward it's turned out exactly the way you feared.

Jihad Jones and the Kalashnikov Babes
By Yussef El Guindi

Cassandra: anywhere from late twenties to early forties; famous actress/star, and acts like one. She also has a down-to-earth side, which comes out in this speech.

Comic

> *Ashraf, an Arab-American actor, is auditioning for a film that he soon discovers is replete with all the worst Arab/Muslim stereotypes. His agent is pushing him to do it because of the high-profile names involved. Ashraf balks, raises objections and holds up the audition. Cassandra doesn't have all day and soon snaps at Ashraf's objections.*

CASSANDRA: So you're miffed you're not playing a boffo character with a great personality and charm to spare. Well, boo-hoo. Excuse me while I break out the tissues for another struggling actor asked to play crap and make it real. What the hell kind of business do you think this is? An academy for the study of human behavior? This is the land of gummy-bears and popcorn, and making out in the back row and leaving a mess for the ushers to clean up. It ain't deep; it's not real, and if you're lucky you get paid a whole lot. *(Holds up her hand.)* Pfft. Shove it. I don't want to hear it. Do you think I got to where I am today because I was picky? I'm a *woman.* Do you know what I get offered as a *woman?* In a business that prizes eye-candy before everything else? Boobs and ass before character and content? Honey: The pickings are slim. I get my choice of whores, skanks, saints or virgins. Or bitches. Or warrior princesses with penis envy. Or any combination of the above. The trough is full of swill, hon, and always has been, and if you're lucky you find one or two great nuggets in your career and that's what you live off while you forage through more trash. I know my part isn't great. But I'm going to give it everything I have and make those pimply kids in the back row stop tonguing and give me their full sex-crazed attention because goddamn it I deserve it. And if you've got anything in you, you'll take this part and do the same. Jesus. You're an actor. Act like one you little pissant.

Sueño
By Scott McMorrow

Lorna: thirty-six, homeless mother to a ruthless female gang leader (G-Girl)

Dramatic

> *The streets of San Francisco's Mission District are rough. And Lorna should know. She's been living on them since the birth of her daughter, G-Girl. G-Girl has risen to power as a ruthless gang leader. In this scene, Lorna is trying to explain to her daughter that, no matter who is in charge, nothing changes.*

LORNA: It makes me so mad people believin' something's changed with you in charge. Take a look around. You see anything different? Hell no! Last time around it was more of the same crap. I know you girl, I birthed you, brung you into this world. And now you jeffe, big boss of the gangs. But nothing's changed. No matter who's in charge, we get the same shit. People ripping on other people, taking them for whatever they get and leaving nothing. That's the truth of it. They use us up, and when there ain't nothing left, we get tossed in the heap, left to rot bloated in the hot sun like so much garbage. They just as soon fuck you up then feed you around here. Look at you. Thinkin' you actually changin' shit. Ain't nothing changed with you in charge. Killin', stealin', rapin'. Just another fuckin' day in the world, you ask me.

Among Friends and Clutter
By Lindsay Price

Joanne: thirty-five, a single professional woman who doesn't get home much

Dramatic

Joanne sits with her father in the garden of her parents' home. Her father sits in a wheelchair, nonresponsive and basically comatose.

JOANNE: There we are, don't want to catch a cold. But I don't think you'll have to worry today. The sun is so warm. Not hot, just warm. A perfect day. The tulips look great Dad. The colors are so beautiful. Mom said you planted them last year. She thought the frost might have damaged them but they look just fine. Mom looks tired. More tired than usual. I came as quick as I could. I went for a walk this morning, down by the river. Everything has changed so much. Would you believe it, I ran into a girl I went to high school with. She's never left town. Helen . . . funny I can't remember her last name. Anyway she had the most beautiful baby boy with red cheeks and the curliest blond hair you have ever seen.

The house looks a little sad. I think I'm going to go down to the paint store and pick up something for the shutters. You always said that good-looking shutters can hide a thousand flaws. Mom told me you've been like this for a while now. Although she swears you said her name last week. Your face is flushed. Are you feeling the sun, somewhere in there? Are you in there somewhere? Can you see me? This afternoon we'll go to the park and watch the kids play on the swings. As long as it doesn't rain. Would you like that? Would you like to go to the park? Please say something Daddy. Anything. Please.

The Mating Habits of Frogs
By Barbara Lhota and Ira Brodsky

Alison: thirties, an adjunct Creative Writing teacher at the community college

Dramatic

A woman who has been battling breast cancer longs for true intimacy and inspiration from her sister.

ALISON: Well, just hear me. Hear me now. Connect with me through your heart and mind. You're sitting there in that chair, rocking, watching the TV. And I know you love me or you wouldn't have come home with me for every treatment. You make me food and hold my head when I'm kneeling in front of the toilet, but that's not all of what I need. I want you to talk to me tonight. I know you love me, but I need you to tell me that. I need you to say that I'm attractive. That I'm good. That it's not ridiculous to feel interested in some stupid guy like Dr. Dave who flirted with me in the hospital cafeteria today. That it's OK to have cancer and want things for the future. It's OK to have this stupid scar across my chest and be sexy. That maybe sometimes Mom, the martyr of our lives, was wrong. That I will live if I can be brave and take risks and sing out in the pond of love. Will you try?

Couldn't Say
By Christopher Wall

Liz: thirties, phobic, housebound

Dramatic

Ethan was away at work, as usual, the night their son Josh died. He has accused his wife Liz of not doing more to find Josh the night he disappeared. Here Liz tries to make Ethan understand what it felt like to be home that night, alone and scared to leave the house.

LIZ: You don't know what it was like. Gone at a conference, like always. Leaving me with an unruly teenager. Who didn't come home from school Friday. I stood by the phone. Hands clasped. Thinking he'd call. Like he promised he would. And I stood. And stared at that stupid thing. And — and didn't move. I don't remember moving. Don't remember the sun going down. Or sleeping. Or going to the bathroom. Or making a noise. Or hearing a noise. Or seeing a clock. I stood an inch over the phone, eyes on the receiver, and my God, I wanted to scream. I did! And pick it up. Call his friends. People. Anyone I knew. But I was scared. My mind gets away from me sometimes. I know it does. Everyone knows it does. They'd never believe me if I went to them. I found myself Sunday morning. In the corner of the living room. Hugging the phone. Thought maybe I should call the police. You're supposed to call the police. Right? When something bad happens. But I — I couldn't do it. It couldn't be true. Nothing bad happened. I'm not going to call the police, my God, because it can't possibly be true! And while I lay there, Josh had already passed out. Woke. Ate. Found another party. Then wandered onto the highway. No shoes. Or hat. Or jacket. Stoned, aimless, trying to find the house — whatever he was doing, or thought he was doing, it was already too late. He'd been hit. But he came back, see? And told me, so I wouldn't have to worry. Calling the police Sunday wouldn't have changed the outcome. He said it wasn't my fault! He did!

A Bushel of Crabs
By Kathleen Warnock

Julie: thirties

Dramatic

> *Julie is Helen's lover. Helen has invited her old boyfriend*
> *Rich to dinner to ask him if he will be the biological father*
> *of the child she hopes to have with Julie. He's just realized*
> *that Julie and Helen are lovers, and he is inclined to say*
> *"no." Julie is trying to convince him to do it.*

JULIE: I love this woman very much. I would do anything for her.
(Pause.) It's not like *I'm* not scared. It's . . . hard, knowing there's
something that I can't give her. An anonymous donor would . . .
be less threatening. She has a HISTORY with you. I think she
thinks she OWES you something. Do I worry she's still a little in
love with you? Hell, yes! But she wants . . . she thinks you're the
best guy to do it with. And I wonder, if it's going to be possible
to leave it at just that . . . because, you now, if you do it, you're
in our lives . . . forever. You have more of a place in her life than
I do, almost. Always coming around. A kid who looks like you.
(Pause.) I would adopt it, you know. I would be one of the parents. What do you think?

Jello Shot
By Christopher Wall

Sue: thirties, angry, abused, but still has a sense of humor

Dramatic

> *After years in an abusive relationship, Sue finally decides to*
> *move out and leave Joey, her boyfriend of many years. As*
> *she talks to him about where she might go, she reveals how*
> *her mother turned a blind eye to what was really going on*
> *between the two lovers.*

SUE: Mom's? God, no. I'd never go there. She always sides with you.
Last time she came I swore I wouldn't talk about you. Or me. Or
anything. I was so nervous. Keep going from the table. To the
counter. To the fridge. To the table. Coffee. Milk. Mug. My lips.
Each time I turn away, they're saying things — The last thing I
want them to do! — About how you come back, after I kick you
out. Change the locks. Leave for work. You watch me go, break
a window, go through the nightstand, and swipe my condoms.
And when I ask you about it you say — you say you DON'T
WANT ME USING THEM. Can you believe!? A hundred-dollar
window. For a three-dollar pack. Like I can't get them at work.
At a discount. Like I'd run out. After giving you the boot. Bring
back a stranger. Cause I need to — Cause I need to FUCK. When
I'm tired, past tired, of being touched, talked at and — and want
to be alone. I, ugh, must have dropped the sugar. Cause I'm
bending down when Mom says, "You should have kids by now."
That's it. "You should have kids by now." And I sit across from
her. Mug in hand. By a broken window. And realize I have
exactly what I want. I'm alone.

The Wars of Attrition
By Suzanne Bradbeer

Arabella Ferguson: late thirties, attractive, desperate to keep up appearances

Seriocomic

Arabella has had a long hard day at work. She is confiding to her son George.

ARABELLA: Do I look shabby to you? I think I look so shabby. My clothes are shabby. They are. I hardly have anything decent to wear to work anymore. Everything, everything is fraying, or stained, or, out of style at best. I'm supposed to look good for my customers, it's part of my job, right, I'm supposed to look like someone you'd want to trust with your appearance . . . A lady came in after lunch today, I'd just put lotion on my hands, they're so dry this time of year, and here she is, and me with greasy lotion on my hands, but she's in a hurry, not a nice woman you could tell, with her mink coat and rush-rush-rush; so I get the foundation she's asking about, high up on the shelf of course, it's always like that with those people somehow, but I get it, smiling, chattering like I don't know what. And my hands are still slippery because I didn't dare take the time to fully rub in the lotion with Madame staring at me like the Medusa, so of course it slips, the crummy bottle slips, does some wild acrobatic flip, ass over Tacumseh — and 'boom!' 'crash!' there it is, shattered on the marble counter. It was almost worth it because the Medusa jumped back screaming about her precious coat — it was a hideous coat, if you're going to spend that kind of money — but anyway, the foundation was all over *me* not her, all over my best dress. Which is now soaking downstairs in our crummy, shabby apartment. I couldn't stand to look at it another minute. *(She opens her coat, shows her dress.)* This is practically the only decent outfit I have left, does it look shabby to you?

Mornings After
By Kate Monaghan

She: a contemporary woman who ages from her twenties into her fifties during the play. She could be anywhere between thirty and fifty when this event occurs.

Dramatic

> *The play is about important conversations between She and her husband that take place the "morning after" some significant event in their lives. In this scene, it is the morning after she has found a lump in her breast and seen the first doctor about it. It is also a time when their relationship is extremely strained, and communication is very bad between them. He enters, and finds her sitting up in bed and rechecking the lump.*

[HE: *You're handling this well.*]

SHE: Oh, that's just the Me you see. She's busy handling all the logistics of finding out what it is. She's so distracted making doctor's appointments and getting time off from work to keep them — without broadcasting to everyone she works with that she may have cancer, for God's sake — she doesn't have time to get upset. There's another Me over there *(Indicates SR.)* sitting in the corner in the dark. Gibbering. She's afraid of dying, and afraid of how much it will hurt to *not* die. She's afraid of chemo, and of being bald and nauseated. She's afraid of being mutilated. Then, there's the Me over in that corner. *(Indicates SL.) She's* in denial. *(Picks up magazine, flipping through, then pointing to marked article.)* This can't happen to her. She has a mammogram every year. She breast-fed her babies for six months. There's no breast cancer in her family. This is all just going to be a false alarm, and she'll be finished with it this afternoon.

Lie Down with Dogs
By N. M. Brewka

Harriet: mid-twenties to mid-thirties

Dramatic

> *Harriet and her dead brother Robbie's lover Walter are try-*
> *ing to sell off Robbie's possessions at an outdoor flea mar-*
> *ket on a freezing cold New England Sunday morning.*

HARRIET: If Robbie could see us now, he'd die laughing. We're like a
couple of ants trying to con the other stupid ants into lugging
away the crumbs of Robbie's crummy life, and don't you give me
that whipped puppy look, Walter, because I am not buying it,
just like nobody's buying all this pathetic crap. I'm not blaming
you for Robby's death, nobody is, but couldn't you at least have
found an indoor flea market, for God's sake? Someplace warm
where there would have been at least a chance of selling something? We can't pack all of this stuff back up again, Walter. Look
at it all! It would be like, like trying to vacuum up his ashes and
stuff them back in the jar.

Razing the 'Rents
By Cynthia Franks

LucyAnn: thirty-one, pretty, but insecure especially in the presence of her mother

Dramatic

> *LucyAnn is speaking to her mother, Twila, who has found the track trophy Lucy won in high school and put it on top of the television. She dusts it and mentions how she went to Lucy's track meets. The trophy is an open wound to Lucy. When she won it Twila told everyone, "It's the coach's award. The trophy they give the slow people." Now Twila suddenly goes on and on about how proud she is Lucy won it fishing around for Lucy to say she is a good mother. Lucy can't take it anymore.*

LUCYANN: It would have been a good time, if only you'd have sat quietly in the bleachers like the other parents; but no, you couldn't sit in the bleachers like the other parents. Not my mother, no, you had to stand in the parking lot and yell, "Go lead ass!" Isn't that funny! "Go lead ass!" I know it's funny. Go on laugh. It's funny. Hilarious. All the other kids thought it was funny. Go lead ass . . . I ran the two-mile. Do you know what that took? Eight times around the track and each time I pass the second turn my mother stands on the hood of our station wagon and yells at the top of her lungs, GO LEAD ASS! Ha, ha . . . Yeah, you're a real laugh riot. I tried to ignore it. I'd concentrate on the sound of my feet on the cinder track, crunch, crunch, crunch; but I can't drown it out. My friends thought you were cool. For the rest of high school I was lead ass. I tried so hard . . . Go lead ass! IT'S NOT FUNNY TO ME, MOM! Why did you do that? Do you have any idea how that made me feel? Any at all? Huh? What were you thinking? DO YOU HAVE ONE LOVING BONE ANYWHERE IN YOUR BODY? JUST ONE? I HATE YOU! *(Pause.)* I don't hate you. I — It's still not funny to me.

Red Light, Green Light
By Erik Patterson

Becky: thirty-one years old, a stripper, has a sixteen-year-old daughter

Dramatic

> *Becky and Kristen have been lovers for the last six months.*
> *They met at a strip club, where they both work; they moved*
> *in together almost immediately. The last few weeks have*
> *been tough on them — Becky's brother Elliot was gay*
> *bashed and her sixteen-year-old daughter Rose gave birth a*
> *month prematurely. Becky and Kristen are at the hospital.*
> *Becky just found out that they get to take her grandson*
> *home today, and Kristen just told her that Elliot's being*
> *released as well. Here, Becky breaks up with Kristen.*

BECKY: Don't touch me. Stop it, OK? Just stop it. I don't want you to touch me. I need some space, OK. Please. I'm sorry, Kristen. I love you. But I'm about to crawl out of my skin. My little brother Elliot's OK. And my new grandson's OK. So now I'm gonna go. I just need to disappear, OK? I need to get away from you, and my family, and the strip club — I just need to get away from everything. I don't want to talk. I don't want you to try to stop me. I don't want you to say anything that will make this harder than it is. I don't know where I'm going. I don't know if I'm coming back. I just need to figure out a lot of things. I don't expect you to understand. But would you tell Rose that I love her and I wish I could be a better mother? And would you tell the rest of my family that I'm sorry for running away again? And tell my mom it's not about her. And tell Elliot that I hope he understands that I love him, that this isn't about him, and I waited until I knew he was gonna be OK. And if Rose starts to forget that I love her, would you tell her I love her again? And just — could you do all that? I love you too, Kristen, I love you too. And I hope that someday you can still love me. I just — I don't want to be touched. I've been touched my whole life. And I can't — I just don't want to be touched anymore. So . . .
(Becky exits. Kristen stands there alone for a beat. Lights shift.)

The Mandible
By Elaine M. Hazzard

Eloise Tarragon: opera diva, late thirties

Comic

*Eloise describes the sudden demise of her husband while at
dinner in a restaurant in Central Park two weeks earlier.*

ELOISE: Not at all, my dear Penelope, your instincts about eating
bones with the fingers may not be an interruption at all, but
instead an untimely and bitter revelation. If only I had thought
to suggest utensils! I had no intuition of disaster. No prescient
sense of impending destiny. No thought of ruin! Like an ingénue
my thoughts were of the peonies, my new bracelet from Harry
Winston and my beloved Constantine. But then! The rib rises to
my darling's lips. He chews it. He is feeling playful. I remind him
of the rib that was taken from Adam to create Eve. He adopts a
Bohemian air and gnaws at the bone with abandon. He bites!
Something is wrong! He chokes, he stoops, he falls sideways,
sending the wine bucket flying. I am up but my gown is in the
way; the waiters reach him before I do. "Constantine!" The
maitre d' is there and administers the Heimlich maneuver with
fortitude, intent on saving his patron. Constantine turns red and
blue and the ambulance is called and we are at Grand Mercy
Hospital. But there is no mercy.

Lucy Devil Has Wealth Syndrome
By Chris Howlett

Lucy Devil: mid to late thirties, extravagant movie star extraordinaire

Seriocomic

> *Lucy explains to her estranged sister, Penny, why she has*
> *been allowing her live-in help, Samantha, and her manager,*
> *Teddy, to "skim a little off the top" of her earnings all these*
> *years.*

LUCY: Oh, yes. It's supposed to matter, isn't it? In your "real" world.
But why should I care? I have lots of money. I have wealth syndrome. *(Beat.)* Teddy and Samantha don't make me live here. I
choose to live here with Samantha. Would you care to know
why, sister? *(Penny says nothing.)* Precisely because it isn't real.
Personally, I've never seen the attraction of the "real" world. In
my experience it's ugly and stinky and full of dubious types.
(Beat.) It makes me dry retch in the same manner as those labo-
rious family celebrations. *(Lucy turns to Teddy and Samantha.)*
But these two! My little children. The hoops I make you
jump through! The trials I inflict! I must be terribly hard work,
what with the mood swings and the tantrums and the rampant
food allergies. *(Beat.)* I can understand why they would want a
little something extra for the trouble. *(She turns back to Penny.)*
Do you understand, Penny? I've always wanted to live in a
dream. That's what my emotionally stunted family never under-
stood. And why shouldn't I? *(Beat.)* I think you've always
wanted to live in a dream, too. But you were never brave
enough. *(Beat.)* They make me feel safe. Who cares why?

Possums
By Keith Huff

Veronica: twenties to thirties

Seriocomic

> *Veronica speaks to Brad on an idling commuter train. Years ago, they were an item . . . until Veronica, pregnant with Brad's child, opted to have an abortion without telling Brad for the sake of her acting career.*

VERONICA: I was up for a Woody Allen movies two weeks ago. This close. I did the craziest thing, Brad. For my audition, I was so freaked, I didn't prepare a thing. Major big deal, so I used reverse psychology on myself. Instead of driving myself apeshit preparing, I did nothing. Nada. Not one thing. Audition time comes, I'm front and center: me and Woody. Monologue time and I've got squat. So I prayed. Song of Bernadette time. *(She unleashes a soaring operatic note to the heavens.)* Whatever words God puts in my mouth, I run with it. I was a woman possessed, Brad. Exit Jennifer Jones, enter Linda Blair. I babbled a mile a minute. Ten minutes straight. I laughed, I cried, and everything in between. So did Woody. He was floored, Brad. Knocked flat. He told me: "Don't move! I'll be right back!" The producers, it turns out, were out front smoking. Woody drags them back in to meet me. Introductions: How are you, how are you, nice tits, you're beautiful. Then Woody asks me to do my monologue again. I tried, but I was used up. Spent. The Coke machine was empty and out of change. I prayed again. But nothing, Brad. I came with nothing, I had nothing. This close. *(Laughs and wipes tears from eyes.)* This New Rochelle show I'm in's not bad. Not great, but not bad. The Dick Van Dyke crowd laps it up. If it gets decent reviews, they might bring it into the city.

High Noon
By Jo J. Adamson

Sally: late thirties, an aging singer/dancer

Comic

> *It is three o'clock in the morning and Sally suffers from night terrors (a malady where you wake up suddenly, talk incoherently and you're terrified of something you can't see). Sally is afraid to go to bed because she fears she'll wake up with another episode. To keep herself awake she sits at her makeup mirror and fiddles with her makeup. She has come to terms with the fact that she'll never be a Broadway star or pick up a Tony, but she is determined to continue working in a business that has little room for an aging woman in musical comedy.*

SALLY: I went from playing the star's best friend to playing someone's mother. Over night! "Do I look different to you?" I demanded of my agent. "Where on my face am I old enough to have a twenty-three year old kid?" He mumbled something about our "national obsession with youth." I said that Mrs. Patrick Campbell played Liza Dolittle well in her fifties and he said that I wasn't Mrs. Pat and he wasn't George Bernard Shaw. And did I want the part or not? *(Sally picks up makeup brush. She lightly strokes her cheek with blusher.)* I quote George Eliot to him. "A woman can hardly choose . . . she is dependent on what happens to her. She must take meaner things, because only meaner things are within her reach." "I'm not him either," he says. I point out that George Eliot was not a him but *her.* He said that he don't care if her is a speckled mongoose. He's scheduled an audition for ten o'clock and if I don't go home and get some sleep, I'd be able to play the part of the *grandmother.*

Rapture
By Ruth Tyndall Baker

Carol: best friend of a woman who has cancer.

Seriocomic

> *Carol has brought gifts to cheer up her friend who has cancer.*

CAROL: Well, you have to get ready for the big event, wear something really special, because you, my dear friend, if you have to spend any time in the hospital and go through any of that, that dreadful shedding of your locks, you are going to be the sexiest bald babe that Jack has ever seen, and he won't even notice the — Well, anyway, close your eyes! Go on, close your eyes! Now picture this. You're sipping tea on the veranda while your scrumptious Jack walks down the lane lined with Magnolia trees toward the "plantation." As he draws closer, he notices that his beautiful wife is no longer wearing a peaches-and-cream gown befitting an innocent southern belle but — something that brings out the beast in him! *(Miming taking from box a wig and putting it on her friend.)* This beautiful Marilyn Monroe wig! Wa-wa-wa-WA! And . . . *(She sprays perfume.)* . . . a little whiff of magic! *(Giggling.)* Of course, you shouldn't wear anything else with the wig! *(Beat.)* You, you look just fine, Maryann. Just fine. You're going to be just fine. *(Beat.)* And I'm going to be right here with you for now. I'll go to the doctor with you when Jack can't go. And I'll make tea for you, and hold your hand, and I'll stay until you make your decision about the surgery . . . or afterward . . . or until you send me away.

Mercy Falls
By Jeni Mahoney

Wanda: thirties, a writer of inspirational books

Seriocomic

> *Wanda reveals her secret to her fan and visitor Marcy:*
> *Although well, she stays in the hospital because the woman*
> *in the next bed is channeling the philosopher Martin Hei-*
> *degger.*

WANDA: I haven't told the doctors. Don't you get it, Marcy? Martin
Heidegger doesn't want to talk to the doctors, he wants to talk
to someone with more experiential . . . experience. Someone who
is working daily on approaching life from an authentic-being-
toward-the-world place. I have the kind of philosophical web-
bing that a doctor cannot possibly have. You must be able to see
that, being an artist yourself.

[MARCY: *Oh. Yes, of course.*]

WANDA: Of course, of course. That woman is channeling Martin Heidegger! Do you think it is just a coincidence that she is in the bed
next to mine. No, no Marcy, there is no such thing as coincidence. Chance? Ha! Chance is the hobgoblin of a chaotic mind.
Something happens to you, Marcy, and I bet you ask "Why is
this happening to me?" — don't you?

[MARCY: *Sometimes.*]

WANDA: It's not why things happen, but what is it that is happening.
Half of the answer is knowing the right question. The question
is not, "Why am I in a room where a woman is channeling Martin Heidegger?" I trust that the world has its reason for such
things. The real question is, "What is Martin Heidegger trying
to tell us?" Hmm? *(With much gravity.)* "What?"

Fear and Loathing on the Nile
By Suzanne Bradbeer

Margot: thirties, a long-suffering actress who finally got a break

Comic

> *Margot has the role of Cleopatra in Shakespeare's* Antony
> and Cleopatra. *She's been slogging away at a career for years
> and this is the best role she's ever had. Here she is con-
> fronting Merrie who performs as one of Cleopatra's hand-
> maids in the play. It is after the opening night performance,
> and Merrie, young and eager, has just stolen Cleopatra's
> death scene. Margot is furious as she confronts her, but is
> desperately trying to be a "good person" and maintain her
> composure.*

MARGOT: Uh. Merrie. There *was* one little thing about tonight. Since
you asked. Just one little, issue. You know in the last scene where
we all get, where we all die — please don't cry again. You're very
sad of course — as the *character* — but your reaction, it just, it
seems a little out of proportion. Look at Iras. When she dies,
plonk, she's dead. Don't you think she's just as sad as you are
that Cleopatra dies? She's heartbroken, of course, but there's no
drama, no flinging herself around the palace. Just Dead. Very
sad, bye-bye forever, Iras. Now it is true that, as you say, you die
last. But that does not mean that the play is about you. No.
Don't get me wrong, you're very important and there are no
small roles and all that blah-blah-blah, but the play is about me.
And Antony. So when you're dying and heaving yourself all over
the stage, it takes focus away from, well, me. And what the play
is really about. See tonight, your grief was *bigger* than Cleopatra's and that doesn't make sense, do you see what I'm saying?
In the context of the story? So all I'm asking is that my death
scene be my death scene — now is that really too much to ask?
Is that so very selfish? Because when you get right down to it,
I'M the Queen of the Goddamn Nile, OK? And the play is called
Antony and Cleopatra, not Antony and Charmian-the-the-the
who are you?! Why are you blubbering about Galileo??? It's called
Antony and *Cleopatra.* Cleopatra, Cleopatra, *CLEOPATRA!!!*

To Mrs. Robinson
By Barbara Lhota and Ira Brodsky

Amelia: early thirties

Comic

> *Amelia, early thirties, has begun dating a much younger man. In this speech, she explains to her friend Liza the reason she's not sure she can keep dating him.*

AMELIA: Well, we were at Tony's, waiting in line. And I saw this patron, this older woman, get pinched by this teenage boy. Tim didn't notice at all. He was putting our names in. This patron let out a little scream, but then she looked pleased. I was disgusted! Like "Oh my God, she's a pervo" and then I thought momentarily, "Oh my God. Am I a pervo?" Then I brushed it aside. Anyway, that's the background. Then we got a great seat near the window. Tim looked great. He had on a nice comfortable, well, tight black shirt and new blue jeans. And it was very casual and romantic until he brought up *Raiders of the Lost Ark*. He just saw it on cable one night for the first time. I said, "I remember seeing that in the movie theater with my brother. I loved it!" He was like, "Wow, that would have been so great to see that in the theater." And then I realized he must have been too young. And I said, "Now, I'm feeling like Mrs. Robinson." And he said, "Who?" OK, so he didn't know *The Graduate*. But then I started doing math. Not just *The Graduate,* even movies like *Raiders of the Lost Ark*. It turns out it was two years before he was born. Then he brings up *Breakfast Club*, which of course was 1982, the shining movie of my twelve-year-old life. And he says, "I love those old movies from the 80s." Old movies, he says. Old movies echoes. I realize he was two when that came out. He doesn't even remember regular roller skates or Wham's breakup. Heck, he doesn't remember George Michael! I start counting things. I'm thinking, "Oh my God! He only remembers *Family Ties* and *Dynasty* from reruns, if at all. He's probably never even seen *The Brady Bunch* or *Dance Fever*. Not that that's a bad thing really. He was two years old when *Romancing the Stone* and *The Terminator* came out. Oh my God. I *am* the pervo!

Last Love
By Peter Papadopoulos

Lucida: late twenties to early thirties, an assertive, successful
businesswoman

Seriocomic

> *Lucida and Charles are separating from their marriage.*
> *Charles calls to close their local telephone service account,*
> *but when he refuses to tell a convenient white lie to the cus-*
> *tomer service representative, Lucida is forced to put down*
> *the large pile of items she is packing, pick up the phone, and*
> *close the account herself. She hangs up the phone and*
> *explodes at Charles.*

LUCIDA: She wouldn't have known you were lying!
  She wouldn't have had the foggiest idea
  that some
  pudd-spanker,
  some
  Ghandi-wannabe,
  had just broken his solemn vow
  never to lie to a telephone service representative!

  She would have gone home from work,
  changed into her slutty leather skirt,
  gone out to the bar,
  struck out with all the good-looking businessmen,
  struck out with all the *bad*-looking businessmen,
  and gone home with Ugly Larry again —
  the same as always!

  She wouldn't have known!
  It wouldn't have changed her life!
  (Pause.)
  You don't like to lie because you think it makes you a good per-
  son.
  Maybe if you just thought of yourself as a decent person

— which you're not —
but if you did,
maybe you WOULD be a good person.
Good enough to stomach an occasional bona fide LIE.

Instead, you staunchly hold the high ground —
this kind of lie is OK and I can do it and still be a good person,
and *this* kind of lie is not OK and I look down my nose at people who do it — who aren't following my moral pie chart.

That's how it is to be loved by you —
to be a part of some grand karmic test you are always filtering the world through.

Your love
is like sucking dirt through a straw.

Fast Friends
By Adrien Royce

Rhonda: thirties, an unhappily married freelance writer

Dramatic

> *Elizabeth Narasaki is a college professor of psychology.*
> *Rhonda and Elizabeth go to a series of movies and plays*
> *over a two-week period. They become best friends only to*
> *discover they're not a match at all. And still Rhonda is des-*
> *perate for Elizabeth's approval/love.*

RHONDA: What relationships have you been in, Elizabeth? Relationships with people you disdained. People who were never quite up
to your standards? People you were grading. People who you
could discard — except for the one in Washington. Alan, or
whatever the hell his name really is — Alan who you can "never
get enough of," who you haven't seen for two years. *(Rhonda
grabs some of the reviews and maps.)*

So, what's my grade, Elizabeth?! Go ahead. You can tell me.
Don't worry I won't take "umbrage." *(Elizabeth is not going to
leave without picking up all of her scattered reviews and maps
and money.)*

You know, Elizabeth, all I wanted to do was vent a little.
You know "I vent, therefore I am." So much for having a psy-
chologist for a friend. *(Elizabeth continues picking up all of her
scattered restaurant reviews and maps.)*

You know, Ms. Narasaki, now that I've given this some
careful thought and consideration — *(Rhonda picks up eyeglass
case. Rhonda puts on Elizabeth's glasses. Rhonda pretends to be
Sigmund Freud. German accent; clinical.)*

I believe, Ms. Narasaki, I believe, you are a woman who is
looking for another woman. No, not for sexual gratification.
Most certainly not. You would never have courage enough for
that — though that is something we can most certainly discuss
at a later date — no, I believe you are simply searching for
women you can reject. Just as your mother rejected you. With
her silence. And this new friend Rhonda Eisenberg, is that her

name, Ms. Narasaki. Yes, I believe that is her name. This new friend Rhonda has provided you with yet another woman for you to reject. And might I add, a nice touch to have rejected a Jewish woman. Very nice touch. *(Rhonda takes off glasses. Rhonda calmly places glasses back in an eyeglass case.)*

And I'm happy to oblige you, Elizabeth. But what do I get out of this? What need of *mine* are *you* going to fill?

Hurricane Iris
By Justin Warner

Nell: a rabbi, late twenties to early thirties

Seriocomic

> *Nell, a female rabbi, has come to Florida to pay respects to her mother, Iris: an acerbic, manipulative, anti-religious battle-axe who claims (falsely) to be terminally ill. Possessive of Nell and contemptuous of marriage, Iris does everything she can to scare off Nell's newly converted, snowboarding fiancé, Louis. When Nell confronts Iris, she claims to be doing Nell a favor. "You can't expect loyalty from a man," Iris warns. "That's why women have children." Nell responds with anger, determination, and defiance.*

NELL: That's not why you had me. You didn't have a reason. I'm just an accident. An unfortunate, unremarkable, untraceable spill in your long line of casual fucks. *(Catches herself. With more composure.)*

I know why I had you though. How I ended up with you for a mother. You are a test. You are a test from God and there's no way I'm going to fail. You want another bitter, manipulative, self-loathing old atheist to keep you company? Well, it's not going to be me. I'm going to honor you the way God intended. I'm going to get married and raise a healthy Jewish family. And when you die I'm going to say Kaddish for you, even if it makes you roll over in your grave. And there's nothing in the world you can do to stop me.

Black Flamingos
By Julius Galacki

Cecilia: "I'll call you . . ." "She who drives." Late twenties to early thirties; tough and fiercely determined, her movements are quick and nimble; she is attractive in an unconventional way, and wears comfortable, clean travel clothes; she is on a quest.

Dramatic

> *In this monologue, Cecilia is trying to convince Jake to join her on her quest to find God and exact revenge on Him. (The ellipsis below indicates a short response from Jake.) They are miles from anywhere, in the Utah salt flats.*

CECILIA: There's a buzzing all the time in my ears, Jake. A drone of locusts chafing their wings. I'm trapped between the earth and the sky. God's a mean son of a bitch — that's what I'm trying to tell you. I've been hearing Him laugh ever since I drove through hell. . . . We were coming back from a wedding — the bride was my little sister. So, there we were, a dozen cars, like a big white elephant honking away. Then time began to slow down for me. I saw it from the start. It was a fuel truck, Jake. Came through the guard rail from the other side. Just like a big hand sweeping away the ball and jacks. I saw my windshield frost and collapse like a thousand icicles. When they fell away, when I could see clearly again, time stopped completely. The flames eating away at a woman in white, froze solid. Up above, there was nothing but stars in front of me and that bastard laughing in my ear. I had just driven straight through the pipe of hell and nothing had happened to me. Not a cut. Not a burn. Nothing. I passed through it all. Through it all. So, do you understand why I drive? I'm looking for Him, Jake. I keep driving and little pieces of Him stick to me like burrs. Like tonight. Little rotting pieces of flesh made in His image. But I know if I keep going, I'm going to see him whole. Like I did that night. Like a mountain stretching up to the stars. And when I find this God again — when I hear him laughing again, I'm going to drive my car right into this throat. It's going to choke him like a chicken bone. I know I can't kill him. But I want to distract him just long enough to give the world some sleep.

The B Side
By Katharine Clark Gray

Regina: twenties to thirties, a club gal, stylish, tough, totally bent

Comic

Regina tells Beth, her roommate, why she's getting home so late.

REGINA: Simon is a shitbag. Lucky for him (he's a cute shitbag), or he'd be dead already. Good looks are just asshole camouflage. He fuckin' — I just got back from the club. Wanna know why? Huh? Because of his coat. His fucking coat. Y'know that clear vinyl trenchcoat he got on St. Mark's? Looks like a full-body condom? . . . Yeah, well, he left it in coat-check and then lost the tag, and they wouldn't give it to him until everyone cleared out for the night. Do you know how long that takes? . . . It's a fucking rave, OK, there's bound to be ten or twelve Tiny-tee losers still on their feet at nine in the morning. We had to wait for every single techno-dork to find the exit before they'd let his jacket go. I mean, he described the fucking thing to the bottom of its pockets, and they're giving him shit about whether it's his? . . .

But get this. Simon's gotta work at nine, right, so he doesn't have time to stick around. So who gets to stay in his place? (If I say no,) right, I can hear him piss and moan for the next week about his new condom coat, and how he just got it, and how much it cost, and how I'm such a worthless bitch because I wouldn't do him one little favor when he buys me so much and does everything I ask him to and I don't love him and he worships me and I'm ungrateful and he's gotta go to work now so will I just shut the fuck up and do this one thing for him?

So I'm going to bed . . . If Simon calls you can tell him I pissed in his jacket.

Lonely Girl
By Cameron Rabie

Melissa: a depressed and frustrated woman in her thirties

Dramatic

Johnny and Melissa have been in a rocky relationship for the last two years of their marriage. They are celebrating their seventh anniversary at some fancy restaurant. What is expected to be a romantic evening ends up being a date from hell. Melissa responds to Johnny telling her to keep her voice down after getting frustrated with her.

MELISSA: You want me to keep my voice down? You never tell her to keep her voice down when you're fucking her, in our bedroom. Let me get your honest opinion. Do you think it's appropriate for our kids to be woken up by screams of "Fuck me harder Johnny?" I come home at seven o'clock every morning from a hard night's work, trying to support my family, and I come home to your tired, cheating ass. And my daughter, no *our* daughter coming up to me and telling me that she heard sounds coming from our bedroom. "It sounded like someone was getting hurt Mommy." *(She laughs.)* She thought someone was getting hurt. Did you hurt her Johnny? Did you screw her twenty-year-old blonde-bombshell's brains out? You want to know what the saddest part is? In our seven years of marriage I don't think I've ever moaned loud enough to wake up the kids. When we got married I vowed to be with you in sickness and health, for richer or poorer. Well I stood by you when you lost your job and I stood by you when you were sick. But I won't stand for this bullshit.

The Abundance
By Paul Heller

Joan: late thirties, a literature professor who can only find adjunct (temporary) positions

Dramatic

> *Joan and Ivan are newly married. Joan thought Ivan wanted to have a child with her and was going to meet her at the ob-gyn office. He didn't show up. Now she finds him in his office going over papers.*

JOAN: We made the appointment around *your* schedule. Schedule from Middle English, meaning a slip of parchment. From the Indo-European root *skei,* to split, and interestingly enough, you'll like this, *scitian,* to shit. Schedule and shit, same root: Would you credence it. Were you delayed reading this paper? Or this one, or this one? I figured out the whole cretinous system. How to call an ob-gyn while I'm simultaneously delivering a lecture on scansion in the Wife of Bathe, how to get one doctor to fax results to another, and all you had to do was show up. Right. Well, we have a year, maybe two. Your sperm's gone funny, my follicles are dodgy. They don't fucking know, Ivan, but *(Tossing Ivan an ovulation kit.)* it's now or not at all. Doctor said, I'm probably ovulating. I've got to piss on it. If it turns blue, we fuck. It takes half an hour. Think sexy thoughts. Are you thinking sexy thoughts? *(Pause.)* That's an awfully long pause. *(Pause.)* So I gather from that pregnant pause that it's "not at all." Six months trying, the miscarriage, these last three weeks waiting for the appointment, that was all what? An expediency? *(Pause.) Expediency.* A contrivance adopted to meet an urgent need: from Latin *expediens,* self-serving. As in expedient, not as in expectant, as I was for three months and will probably not be again. Pregnant with your expediency. *(Pause.)* The doctor said we could have a child. Probably. I'm willing.

Erratica
By Reina Hardy

Dr. Stafford: late thirties, a professor of English. Brilliant, acerbic, rigid and sexy

Comic

Dr. Samantha Stafford has recently made the mistake of sleeping with one of her students, hoping it would cure his hopeless infatuation. Instead, he camps outside her office, writing very bad sonnets and slipping them under the door. Dr. Stafford pretends to be out. She's spent the past eight hours locked in her office, drinking and talking to the ghost of Kit Marlowe. The sonnet count has just reached seventy-two.

STAFFORD: Christ! Go away! Go away, do you hear me? *(She goes to the door and hammers it with her fists.)*

Leave! Go! Exit! Vamoose! Do you think we have a future here? Do you think the fact that we had sex means I love you, or like you, or accept your existence? I can't even look at you. You sicken and revolt me. You make me think of everything I hate about men, students, teachers, the world, myself . . .

I regret last night more than you can possibly imagine. More than any night has been regretted I regret last night. If deus popped out of the machina right now, and gave me a voucher for one trip into the past, can you guess what I'd do with it? The library at Alexandria would burn, every volume unsalvaged. Little Adolf would lie safe, unstrangled in his crib. The name of the Dark Lady would remain a mystery, as would the true origins of the universe, because I'd be, at this moment, rocketing back one day and preventing myself from sleeping with you!

While the Baby Sleeps
By Aline Lathrop

Jasmine: late twenties to early thirties. The stay-at-home mother of
   an infant. Formerly a postdoctoral fellow in Cell Biology.

Dramatic

> *Jasmine and Ted lived very independent lives until the birth
> of their daughter. When the baby was born, Jasmine found
> herself incapable of separation from her daughter and there-
> fore could not return to work. Jasmine's decision to stay at
> home has caused an unwelcome dependence on Ted and
> financial problems. In this scene, Ted is angry that she has
> not restocked the refrigerator with milk, which he views as
> one of her duties since she is staying at home.*

JASMINE: What I decided? You have no idea what I decided.

   I never told you about going to the clinic. I never told you
because it was my decision to make.

   You knew I thought we should be more stable. Wait 'til I got
a faculty position so we'd know where we were going to be in
the long-term. Buy a house in a good school district. Another
two years . . .

   So I went to the clinic. I met with the social worker, signed
the disclosures, took off my clothes, put on one of those tissue
paper gowns, and even put my feet in the stirrups. But then I
took off the gown, put my clothes back on, and walked out of
there. And that was the first thing I ever did in my life that didn't
make sense to me, but it sure wasn't the last.

   No. I didn't change my mind because of you. Not entirely. It
was something else. The same thing that kept me from going
back to work at the lab. And I honestly don't know what that
was. Is. But I do know that what we have here is what you
wanted. Maybe not exactly on your terms, but still. So don't
start ranting at me about milk.

Visions
from *The Food Monologues*
By Kerri Kochanski

Woman: thirties to forties, overweight

Dramatic

> *Woman stands with a piece of chocolate cake. She angrily argues with someone who has just insinuated that she is too fat to eat chocolate cake, and that she needs to watch what she eats. She stands up for her right to be who she is.*

WOMAN: Just because *you* don't believe it doesn't mean I have to stand here and stop doing it . . . People have *beliefs* . . . Beliefs that may be *different* than yours . . . And you shouldn't make other people whose beliefs are different than yours try to change them . . . Change is *not good* . . . Not when it is *forced* by other people . . . *(Thinks.)* Because you *can't force* someone . . . *(Beat.)* You believe what *you* believe . . . *(Suddenly not so certain, shaken.)* And *I* believe what *I* believe . . . Which is *(Suddenly angry.)* Something you cannot just come up to me and *change.* *Change* . . . Because you're trying to trick me? Because you're trying to brainwash me . . . ? Because you're trying to make me be more like you? Because you don't *like* chocolate cake? I *like* chocolate cake . . . And just because you think that a person like me shouldn't eat it . . . Just because *you* think, in your skinny little head . . . *(Beat.)* I have visions . . . And in my visions, I see a person who is big, and fat, and beautiful . . . And most of all — happy . . . Happy because she is eating chocolate cake . . . And because she doesn't have to think about — The ugly things that *you.* That *you* see . . . When you see someone like me . . . Eating chocolate cake — when you force me, to see what you see . . . When you are so blind, *(Begins to sadden.)* that you can't see someone at all.

Queen Bee
By Dennis Schebetta

Pamela: thirties, Vice President of Marketing for a large corporation

Seriocomic

> *Pamela is a high-powered marketing guru working for a*
> *large firm and she wants a baby without any hassle. Jim is a*
> *temp with low aspirations who works in her office. One day,*
> *she calls him in for an unusual proposal — to be the father*
> *of her baby for a large sum. However, his morals and his*
> *girlfriend prohibit him from agreeing to the offer immedi-*
> *ately so Pamela persuades him with her savvy sales skills.*

PAMELA: You're kissing me off, aren't you? What's wrong, five thousand not enough?

[JIM: *You said it wasn't negotiable.*]

PAMELA: This is business. Everything's negotiable. *(Gets out check book.)*

> I can write this check out with a lot of zeros, Jim. What's it going to be? Look, I need someone with no connections. With the boyfriend, it could get complicated. But see, I can't just go to a stranger I meet in a bar — too many risks — so I need someone on the fringe of acquaintance who may be able to stay with the job till it's done, then disappear. A nonentity, if you will. Like a temp. That way, when the child is old enough to want to know who her daddy is, she won't be able to hunt him down. I know the whole idea of hiring someone to make a baby is unusual, but sometimes you have to think outside of the box. The modern world thrives on unorthodox innovations. Where would we be if Bill Gates hadn't stolen that Windows computer system from Apple which in turn stole it outright from IBM? I'll tell you; we'd still be Cro-Magnon man worshipping fire and praying for a good hunt. But no, someone invented the wheel, someone invented e-mail, someone invented Prada shoes! These great giants chose their own morality in order to succeed and survive. I'm giving you the opportunity to choose your own moral

viewpoint, Jim, to mold your life any way that you desire. Don't be "just a temp." Be a leader. *(She holds up the room key.)*

This is your key to freedom of thought. This is the light that will guide you out of that dark cave of ignorance. Take it in your head. Hold it. Feel your destiny. *(Whispers.)*

And the sex will blow your mind.

Jersey
By Hugh Fitzgerald

Connie: thirty to forty, working-class

Seriocomic

> *Connie is from Paramus, N.J., and has taken her ten-year-old nephew, Paulie, to the beach. Connie was told to be back the following day by Paulie's grandparents (Connie's parents). Connie met a man while at the beach and wants to stay another night. She then puts young Paulie into a phone booth and has him try to talk the grandparents into letting them stay longer. The action takes place at a pay phone booth in the back of a restaurant in Seaside Heights, N.J.*

CONNIE: Hey kid you wanna Yoo-hoo or something, I'm gonna call your grandma and get her to let us stay down here another night. We can go for a Philly cheese steak or one of those sausage and onions. That sound good huh? Buh . . . I gotta get this over with . . . What's the thing huh? I can't have a weekend? OK here Paulie . . . you call . . . cuz when you talk she'll feel bad. So let's see . . . I'll dial and when she picks up . . . just start talking real fast. . . . say you're havin' fun . . . the beach . . . you're winnin' some toys . . . Aunt C is feedin' ya . . . you don't wanna come home . . . like that . . . real fast. So . . . she picks up . . . yadda . . . yadda . . . yadda . . . you wanna stay . . . Buh she says no . . . then sniffle . . . sniffle . . . pause . . . wait for her response . . . she stills says no then . . . uh . . . sigh a couple of times and say that you asked me to let you stay another night. Oh and yeah . . . say you met some girl and you're havin' fun . . . you can do it . . . remember to sniffle act like you're gonna cry. If this don't work and she won't let ya . . . shit . . . we're gonna have to blow a gasket on the friggin' car or something . . . I hate to have to pull that . . . buh . . . we ain't goin' back . . . OK so we better call . . . after this we'll go on the boardwalk and get a little beer and something . . . you're a good boy, Paulie . . . a real good kid.

An Unfinished Room
By Mark Rosenwinkel

Naomi: thirties, a radical nun, easily carried away with her passion for social justice

Seriocomic

Naomi is a young activist nun preparing herself for an act of civil disobedience at an animal research site. She speaks to a reluctant middle-aged professor as she equips herself for the protest.

NAOMI: You're damn right you're angry. You can't live in this world without getting angry at something. Look at me. Yes, yes. I can see it. Underneath a thin veneer of inhibition and shyness, there's fire, and passion. Oh, yes, I can see it. You're so full of passion, it scares you and you hide it. But don't worry, you're in good company. Why do you think I'm doing this? I could have gone off, gotten some nice secretarial job. Maybe ended up running some company. What would that prove? People I went to school with, they're all running around in cars and boats, big houses in the suburbs. And here I sit, hunkered down in the dirt, ready to put myself in jail. And why? Because I have passion! And so do you, or you wouldn't be here. Don't be ashamed. Revel in it! I mean, who do you think Christ was anyway, some anemic white guy on sympathy cards? He was a firebrand, a rebel, a man of ultimate passion. The saints, they speak of being ravished by Him. Do you hear me? Do you follow me? They imagined themselves actually being taken up by this, this power, this driving, divinely passionate force . . . You understand me, don't you? There's all kinds of crap that's going on in the world, and I've got to do something about it. It's like a craving, an insatiable drive . . . *(Suddenly looking up.)*

    Here they come. Lie down! If they give you any trouble, kick them right where it counts. We shall be the thorn in their flesh, the obstacle in their side! Come on now! No turning back! NO TURNING BACK! . . . *(Sings.)* "We shall, we shall, we shall not be moved . . ."

Tweaking
By Barbara Lhota and Ira Brodsky

Helen: thirties, an outgoing, strong-minded saleswoman for a large firm

Comic

Helen tries to convince Gina to be her cohort in an elaborate scheme designed to enhance both of their love lives.

HELEN: It's not lying! It's tweaking. It's enhancement of potential truths that would be different if they were. See? When you and I get up to go to the bathroom, we spend a long time there, pretending we're in a long line, which we probably won't need to pretend. Ha! See? Not lying there. The guys start talking about things. Gorgeous Man . . . Flower Man . . . their lives . . . their beautiful, very intelligent, very successful women. I've already instructed Mike to bring up marriage talk with Greg. Come on, with the look. This isn't coercement, it's persuasion, it's intimidation. *(Gina begins to speak. Helen stops her.)* Uht. This leads to how lucky they are. How desirable we are . . . and then Mike and I go home, and he gets all jealous and whiny, thinking my new haircut was in response to Gorgeous Man's flirting. He's feisty. We make up. It's hot. He loves me madly. And you go home with Greg. He stews about Flower Man's flirtation. And he asks you to marry him next weekend. *(Gina gives her a look.)* Fine. So if it doesn't work out with Greg, I got you a date with Flower Man.

Painting by Numbers
By Dennis Schebetta

Jane: twenties to thirties, an attractive businesswoman

Seriocomic

> *Jane is at the Museum of Modern Art with her best friend, Wes. She suspects that her husband is having an affair with his girlfriend, but she is still coming to grips with the idea of finding out the truth, or remaining ignorant.*

JANE: I've been thinking a lot about the idea that ignorance is bliss. I mean, sometimes it's just better not to know. For instance, the government could be theoretically hiding information — I mean, true honest-to-God *facts* — about people being abducted by aliens and used for scientific experiments. We all think it's crazy because life is easier to deal with if we accept that logic. But what if I met some FBI guy like Fox Mulder who disclosed verified government documents to me, or brought me to an actual alien spaceship, showed me a dissected human being on a table, and otherwise had me totally convinced — what would I do? I'd crumble in a heap, shocked by this overdose of knowledge. And yes, a part of me wants to know the truth about David cheating on me. But, I have a good thing going here so why should I mess with it? I shouldn't, and neither should you. Relationships are like art. They simply exist as a thing of beauty.

Riot Standard
By Katharine Clark Gray

Lani: mid-thirties, an aging punk, intense and uncompromising

Seriocomic

> *Lani and her hetero-life-partner Toph are New York City expatriates who now run* The Riot-Standard, *an underground newspaper in an "unenlightened town." Having just made up from a life-shaking fight, Toph asks Lani if she thinks their adopted home really needs the free press. Here Lani works to convince him their efforts are not in vain.*

LANI: Such a question, pet! . . . There is a scene here. It's still underground . . . Hence the term "underground scene" . . .

Look. No one felt more hopelessly trapped than I did as a kid in the 'burbs. Fifteen years old, no car, no art house, I was weird 'cause I didn't like soccer . . . I got lucky. If it weren't for British fanzines and, and reprints of *The Berkeley Barb* and the little xeroxed handouts this punk from my copy shop kept by the register, I wouldn't have known it all existed. The World Outside. The Screaming Free Press. Music to stomp my combats to and words my fists could swing at Aaagh! You know!

But I had to hunt and hunt that stuff. Harder to find than a black person on our block . . .

It starts with being cool. That's how you get them interested. People with riot inside . . . No one starts with Free Mumia.[1] They start with Manic Panic[2] and obscure bands they can name-drop. But one day they turn the page and read landlord conspiracies and racial profiling in schools and their precious Pizza Hut framed by its own garbage and maybe they learn something along with when Fugazi's[3] playing next. So do they need *Riot* here? Sure as shit after coffee and bran.

---

[1] The movement to release journalist and Death Row inmate Mumia Abu-Jamal from prison, on the grounds he was falsely convicted of killing a police officer.

[2] A brand of hair dye famous for its shades not found in nature.

[3] Washington, D.C. band co-founded and fronted by former Minor Threat member Ian MacKaye. The band is self-managed and release all of their material through their own independent label.

Privates
By Janet Allard

Wendy: twenties to thirties, a nurse

Comic

> *When Joe, a movie star and the local candidate for sheriff (and Wendy's ex-boyfriend), comes into the hospital for a penis enlargement, Wendy tries to persuade her co-worker and best friend, Candice, to leak the secret to the press.*

WENDY: *(Wendy, a nurse, pokes her head out of her curtains. Whispers urgently.)* Psst. Candice! What's he in for?
(Wendy opens her curtains. She smokes a cigarette in the supply closet.)
I know it's confidential. But you can tell me, right?
You look stressed. Is it life threatening? His heart?
(Wendy grabs the file from Candice.)
ELEVEN INCHES! He wants to make it 11 INCHES! Is that possible? With what he's got? Can they do that? Do you know how big this is, Candice? This would ruin his fucking career. Do you realize, people would DIE to know this. PAY to know this. THE PRESS — It's HUGE. NEWSWORTHY. This is the only way, Candice. That dickhead's gonna fucking win the election because his daddy's WHO HE IS. Their whole family is gonna rule the whole fucking world from top to bottom, from the guy who makes the laws to the guy who fries you in the chair. This is just the beginning, first it's sheriff, then mayor, then governor of "Kalifonea," and then when he's got the whole world tied around his finger he's gonna run for president of the fucking United States. It's not an election it's a fucking popularity contest. And you have the power. Right here. You're holding it in your hands. This hits the papers and he's out, down for the count, nobody's gonna vote for a small-dick sheriff — no matter who his daddy is or what action movies he's starred in, it would be an embarrassment to our country. Are you gonna let THEM take over the world or are you gonna stop them, DO SOMETHING! Are you gonna call the press, or am I?

Erratica
By Reina Hardy

Lisa Milkmin: thirties, a publicist. She makes an especial point of smiling after each sentence she speaks.

Comic

Professor Samantha Stafford has just completed her scholarly book on Shakespeare. Publicist Lisa Milkmin wants to punch it up for the market, but her client is less than friendly. In fact, the two women hate each other. Here, Lisa outlines her marketing strategy.

LISA: That's a . . . selling point. You're edgy, you've got attitude, you're saying something different. And you've got lots and lots of sex. That's sexy, that sells. And *(A pause to savor.)* You're a woman.

That's why you can get away with it. It's empowerment. Not romantic, not afraid to stand alone and maybe show a little leg. It could be Shakespeare for the Cosmo girl. I think I could get you a spread. But there are still a few problems. Book itself — very highbrow, very clever, kind of hard to read. Funny but smart. Now, I can't ask you to get rid of smart, but we can toss something else in there to lighten the batter. Anyway, here's my strategy. It's two pronged. Play up the women thing. In two ways. One of them is easy, and that's you. Because you are very pretty, you know? In a sort of Mrs. Robinson way. Makeup, spectacles, stilettos. Schoolteacher as sex object. Men will want you, women will want to be you. But they can't, so they'll buy your book. But I don't just want them to buy it. I want them to recommend it to their friends. Fat chance if it's just a lot of rehashing Shakespeare with funny bits. No. New material is key. New female material is key. Sexy new female material. And Sam, you are going to be so proud, cause I have found you just the thing. It's right here at this very institution. Your very own librarian turned it up. The diary of Anna Quinberry, merchant's daughter, lady of the night, fun, fearless, Elizabethan Female! Lost for centuries, found last Tuesday, in her own words . . . Sex in Shakespeare's city! What do you think?

"Will You Please Shut Up?"
By Dan O'Brien

Sylvia: twenties to early thirties

Comic

> *Sylvia and Tom seem to have the perfect relationship: He's a junior investment banker, she's an aspiring writer. But their home life is not nearly as idyllic as it seems . . . And Sylvia's emotions, in particular, have reached their breaking point; she's just thrown Tom's cats out the window, and Tom — ever the victim — would like to know why.*

SYLVIA: — They're not "cats," dear! They're demons! Changelings, hobgoblins, it doesn't matter, *they're evil and they're destroying my life.* I come in here this morning, picture this, me with my cup of coffee, my little nugget of inspiration tucked up in here — I was going to write it today, Tom! The key to my success, Tom! The "story-idea" that was gonna make our life so incredibly unbearably *"nice"!* And there was Pipsy. Or whatever the fuck her name is. With her ass on the keys. Just sitting there, the fat slob, on my typewriter. And I said, "Easy there, Pips, back off now, girl. Momma needs her antique typewriter this morning!" And she gets this look in her eyes, more like in her mouth really, like the Cheshire cat, only more malicious, more sinister, and she starts pressing the keys with her little paw, tic tic, tic tic, in particular the *T,* cause she knows, *the bitch knows* that the *T* is one of the most necessary letters in the English alphabet and if she fucks with my *T* I'm screwed. Ruined. — You know how she gets with chipmunks, mice? Stepping on their tails, letting them go, batting them back and forth? Well that's what she was doing with my *T.* Batting the *T,* batting the *T,* tic tic, tic tic, tic tic tic tic tic — "no Pipsy, no! Let Mommy have the typewriter — *PLEASE PIPSY!"* — and I lunged for the bitch, knocked the wind out of her, knocked the friggin' typewriter off the table too, and before I could even think what I was doing, Pipsy was out the window. *(Beat.)*   And then I threw Ginger out the window too. For good measure.

Hungover from the 80s
By Adrien Royce

Rachel: late thirties, a splendid neurotic approaching one of her many midlife crises

Comic

Rachel is applying for a job. She is talking to the president of the company.

RACHEL: I haven't spoken to my astrologer of nine years since last spring, when I found out that I had the same sign as his mother and he hated his mother! I'm a Libra. But I suppose you don't believe in any of that stuff. You know you can get addicted if you don't watch out. I used to just read the horoscope "once in awhile." In fact, that's the way it started. You know it was fine and dandy when I would innocently pick up the optimistic horoscopes — you know the "you'll meet the amour of your life and find the career of your dreams" stuff. But one day when I was feeling really bad — Dark-Night-of-the-Soul-bad, I knew my only hope was to find some horoscope that could relieve my pain by saying "Yes, you are absolutely right to feel like death today. Don't leave your house. Don't look for work. Don't do anything creative. Don't express love to anyone close to you. Don't fix anything that is broken. Don't pay your bills. And don't, above all, do not, do not put gas in your car because you will be experiencing a change in your mode of transportation. Don't do a bles-sed thing." That usually worked for me. But, then my days were getting worse and worse and I couldn't believe just one horoscope and I had to have another and then another and then another. I would run to the nearest Dominicks or Jewel or Kmart where I could find horoscopes in magazines you'd never even have expected to find them in. And right there between "Clawing Your Way to the Top" and "Orgasms: You Can Never Have Enough of 'em," was Starcast! Ask the Stars for truth and they'll tell you no lie. But, they do lie. They do!

Avenging Grace
By Terri Campion

Meg: a children's writer in her thirties

Seriocomic

> *After surviving a suicide attempt, prompted by a recent street assault and robbery, Meg tries to persuade Marilyn, a stranger who has returned her purse, not to interfere in her next attempt.*

MEG: Marilyn listen to me! I have to believe there's something more for me and I know it's not in THIS world. It's not working for me here. Aren't you hearing what I'm telling you? I just can't seem to connect with anything or anyone for a substantial period of time. And when I do . . . I get so overwhelmed. I screw it up. I say or do the wrong thing, or someone gets hurt . . . or killed. Joey. The night this happened, I was feeling so happy! And strong! Independent! And . . . BAM! Ironic, huh? Just when I feel I'm finally really in the game of life, someone smacks me in the head with a brick. Two times. And the kind of brick the house I grew up in is made of. I'm not a big fan of irony. What else can I say? I just don't have the strength . . . Really. I give up. And I can't live with this creepy feeling . . . this feeling of fear and yearning for death to show up at my door. I want him here already! So, please, Marilyn, I appreciate your concern and all, but really, we barely know each other, so it won't be any big loss on your part. You'll get over me. I promise. So, please . . . don't dump that bleach down the drain. I really need it.

Dangerous Times
By Jean Reynolds

Lenore: late twenties to thirties

Seriocomic

> *Lenore and her husband John live in the country. They have a guest, Walter (an old friend of John's), who has been staying with them for some time. Lenore, having discovered her husband bought a gun, approaches Walter with her concerns.*

LENORE: John bought a gun. Why, Walter? Why would John buy a gun? The John I know wouldn't buy a gun. Have I been married all these years to a man I don't know? You're his best friend. You tell me. Am I getting worked up over nothing? There must be an explanation. For example, bears in the woods. Well, it is isolated up here. All kinds of creatures could be lurking about in the woods. What if a bear lumbered out during a barbecue? I'm sure there's an explanation. Maybe John feels threatened by the world we live in now, all that's happened, all that. Maybe he has need to feel safe from forces we can't predict. Odd, though, he didn't discuss buying the gun with me. Odd. We discuss any major purchase. And I call this a major purchase, don't you? I tell you, Walter, when I saw the gun I felt a chill, yes, a chill. It was last night, during the storm. The lights went out. I brought a candle into John's study, along with his martini. The gun was on the desk. He picked it up. "I'll just put this away until I need it." Need it? Need it for what? Walter, John's not the type to have a gun around. Of course there was that "episode" years ago. That aberration. But nothing since. What if he bought the gun for a . . . a personal matter? A personal matter? Say I'm wrong. Say that, will you? What if he knows about us?

Mercy Falls
By Jeni Mahoney

Marcy: twenties to thirties, a shy, lost soul who thinks she is a jinx

Seriocomic

> *Marcy, believing she is a jinx, panics when the woman in the*
> *next bed dies suddenly during her surprise Christmas Eve*
> *visit to Wanda, her favorite inspirational writer in the hos-*
> *pital.*

MARCY: Don't you get it, Wanda? I'm no good! I'm a jinx. I don't
even know why I'm here! *(Dr. Smitwhistle holds up the medical*
chart.) That isn't even my medical chart! I'm not a patient, I was
just visiting! *(Picks up the tree she had brought in.)* I thought, I'll
just drop off the tree, say hello and be on my way. Easy. What
could be more simple? But no, I can't even give a gift without
tragedy striking. Do you know that when I was ten I accidently
electrocuted my dog, Freckles, with an Easy-Bake oven? And I
used to ask God all the time, "Why me, God, why?" "Don't be
silly, Marcy," God would say, "these things don't happen to you,
they just happen near you." Then he would laugh. And I would
think, is this really God or is it just the inside of my head? And
I figured it must be the inside of my head, either the inside of my
head or, you know, the other one: the bad side. Like a curse. And
every day, every year I wait for a sign — any sign — why. Why?
And now you, Wanda, you come along and tell me that it was
the wrong question in the first place. Well, Merry Christmas
Marcy — now you know the question. "What am I?" What am
I? I am a jinx. I am a magnet for tragedy, and now poor Dr. Smit-
whistle's mother lies dead, yet another innocent victim of
Marcy's curse! Merry Christmas, Dr. Smitwhistle's mother!
Merry Christmas! God Bless Us Everyone!

Paintings
from *The Van Gogh Exhibit*
By Matt Fotis

Erin: late twenties to early thirties, a young mother whose career and
marriage are falling apart

Comic

*A young mother whose career and marriage is falling apart
is in an art museum with her rambunctious young child. She
is waiting for her friend who is an hour late and she is at the
end of her rope.*

ERIN: *(In that motherly whisper/yell.)* Sam. Sam. Get away from the
paintings. Sam!
    (Normal voice, still to Sam.) Fine. Ruin it. I'm sure Van
Gogh won't mind. See what I care. I guess we'll just have to cancel somebody's birthday party.
    (Pause. Screaming.) SAM GET THE FUCK AWAY FROM
THE PAINTING!
    *(Sarcastically to the other mothers staring at her in the
museum.)* Oh yeah, better hide your children from the crazy
lady. Wouldn't want to expose their virgin little ears to the heathen monster. Wouldn't want to expose them to the real world.
Keep 'em locked up in soccer camps and violin lessons their
whole lives so when they grow up they end up giant queers sucking some random guy's cock on a park bench because their dearest mommy fucked them up so bad . . . You do that. Go ahead
and call 'em. You want my phone? I've got night and weekend
minutes . . . Well you know what, why don't *you* go fuck *yourself*? That's right. You heard me.

Meal Ticket
By Kit Wainer

Marcy: early thirties, recent M.A. in English Lit.

Comic

> *Marcy has invited her university friend, Karla, to meet her*
> *for dinner so Marcy can confess that she stole Karla's Mas-*
> *ter's thesis. Karla knows this and has been unwilling to pur-*
> *sue the matter for fear of Marcy going off the deep end*
> *where she so perilously teeters. Marcy speaks rapidly. The*
> *two women are seated in a restaurant. Marcy is having pre-*
> *dinner coffee.*

MARCY: My shrink thinks I need therapy therapy — something other
than therapy. Like a pottery class or line dancing. I think she just
wants to get away from me. It's been twice a week for nine years
except for her Augusts and an occasional sick day. It is a long
time and I'm not a bit better than I was when I started. Of
course, I'm no worse either. And, hell, I can afford it, can't I? But
after nine years I suppose something should have happened or
changed. I think I use her like a journal. I suppose it would be
cheaper to get a notebook. But I know I'd never keep a journal,
too risky. Besides, maybe I'm a secret psycho and if I didn't blow
off steam with my shrink, I'd be a serial killer. No, I'm not the
type. Maybe shoplifting. I do occasionally get the urge to steal
when I'm in a department store. I sometimes even dream I'm
stealing. I never talked about that with my shrink. I don't think
I ever talked about any dreams with her. Aren't you supposed to
talk about dreams with your shrink? I wonder why she never
asks. Isn't she being remiss in her duties? Should I sue her, do you
think? No, I wouldn't want to start all over, too risky. God
knows what I'd say. Maybe I don't need therapy. Or maybe I
should start all over — new shrink, new persona. I might even
tell the new one my stealing dream. What do you think stealing
symbolizes? Of course, a Freudian would say sex, but I prefer
coffee. Ha. Ha. Anyway, what do you think? Do I need therapy?

Missed Connections
By Barbara Lhota and Ira Brodsky

Cynthia: thirties, a well-paid sales rep, wearing a conservative business suit

Comic

Cynthia, the poor woman sitting next to Jackie on a plane, is a frequent traveler and sales rep. She is heading home after a long day of sales meetings. Cynthia tries desperately to avoid talking to Jackie, but as the play progresses, and the flight delay increases, Cynthia becomes more and more fearful about flying and everything else known to man. At this point, Cynthia begins to lose it.

CYNTHIA: I'm not that tall. You'd think I could get comfortable. But I believe they make these seats uncomfortable *on purpose.* They want us to be jealous. So we upgrade to first-class. They give them leg room and comfortable seats. Fluffy pillows and good wine. And they have quiet music for their ears. It's a racket. Because once you've flown first-class, you don't want to go back. It's like getting a demotion. You have a moment of fame and then back to the rat race — the flat Coke and the baby spitting up all over your arm. You ask for a pillow and the flight attendant scoffs. *(Laughs.)* She goes up to first-class and mocks you. "Do you now what that coach passenger asked me for?" *(Laughs, evilly.)* The airplane is the last bastion of the caste system. You're among the peasants now, and you'd better not expect much, lady! When you pass the first-class curtain, you look back longingly. You are impressed and despise them at the same time. They look smug and occasionally guilty, if they're from some place like Oregon, while you are forced to fight over luggage bins in a haze of baby poop. *(Getting louder.)* None of that exists in first-class!

Off Compass
By Kelly Younger

Gayle: thirties, on the verge of a real breakdown or a real break-
through

Seriocomic

> *Suffering from a lack of direction in her life, Gayle missed*
> *her exit home from work and wound up a thousand miles*
> *away at the Graceland Bar in Garden City, Kansas. She talks*
> *into the wee hours of morning with the bartender, Elvis, and*
> *now confesses that the loneliness she thinks she left behind*
> *has followed her here.*

GAYLE: I'm sleepwalking. But if I know I am, doesn't that mean I'm
awake? I can't tell the difference anymore. And I can't hide it. It's
like a birthmark. And I've even read all those *Life's Simple Plea-*
sures–type books and *14,000 Things to Smile About* blah blah
blah. You know that sappy stuff where it says . . . Adopt a
kitty . . . Name your Q-Tips . . . Watch snails make love? But I
don't feel centered. I'm convinced my house is slipping off its
foundation. Really. I can hear it. It creaks and shifts. There's got
to be a crack in the foundation. I can't see it, but I know it's
there. So I crawled under the house one day, just to prove it. Got
down in there with the spider webs and the dirt and cement
and . . . well, after the fire department got me out, I called a con-
tractor to come look for it. So he got down in there, and
searched around with his flashlights and level and all his other
tools, and said, "Nope, sturdy as a brick house." And I said,
"But it is a brick house." "Exactly," he said, and gave me a bill
for two hundred dollars.

Neurotic Splendor
By Adrien Royce

Rachel: thirty-nine years old, novice stand-up comic

Comic

Rachel is talking to an African-American stand-up comic she just met at a comedy club.

RACHEL: *(Ranting; searching for answers.)* True. But no one wants to SEE me be funny. Funny is not very "pretty." Because it's angry. Yup, funny is angry. They don't think I deserve to be funny, uh angry. Maybe they don't think I've ever experienced society's deepest darkest places so that everyone can say, "Sure she's gotta right to be angry. Look what she went through."

Hah, hah, hah. Now we can laugh. Oh, and that jury duty bit of mine you like, "I went for jury duty and they put ME on trial." Yes, pretty funny stuff. You can have it. No, really. I'm sure you'd get a bigger laugh. I'd have to look like *you* to deserve to get a laugh with that joke. But that's because people don't really know how psychotic I become when I get that little perforated notice in the mail. I suddenly have to figure out some way to get out of it. I call therapists I haven't talked to in years to see if I can get letters of emotional instability. I start taking prescription drugs. Stuff like that. *(Builds again to ranting.)*

What IF one day I actually somehow wasn't able to slip out of a jury duty notice?! What if I actually had to go?! I'd totally freak out being around all that government authoritarian testosteronic primitive ME-IN-CHARGE-YOU-DO-WHAT-I-SAY shit! And they *would* end up putting me on trial. Or at least throwing me in jail. I have these terrible fears of being thrown in jail. See, I get caught for everything. Things no one else ever gets caught for. They — whoever the big THEY is — I'm certain they just make up laws when they see me coming. I once got a jaywalking ticket in L.A. for Chrissakes. In L.A. — where nobody walks! How did they even know what I was doing?!

Almost Full Circle at the Guggenheim
By Dianne M. Sposito

Elizabeth: twenties to forties

Seriocomic

> *Elizabeth, a brilliant but extremely shy college professor,*
> *meets a vibrant, somewhat unusual young gentleman,*
> *Quinn, in Central Park. As they get to know one another at*
> *an intimate picnic, the depth of her reticence to love is*
> *revealed as she speaks candidly. (Her words are underscored*
> *with female, plainsong voices.)*

ELIZABETH: . . . how was I a virgin for so long? When I was a kid, every night in summer . . . those velvet Midwestern nights, the breeze on your face, crickets, the heat bugs, fresh tar in the streets to put your toe in and squish, all warm . . . that time was so . . . filled with . . . peace . . . we lived across the street from a cloistered convent with a high retaining wall. Oh, those mysterious ladies behind that wall! After the Angelus bells, I sat on our front porch and waited for the sisters to play volleyball. The sight of their summer white veils and their very white arms reaching for the ball, tender plainsong voices giggling, a flash of face and then a veil. They were so beautiful. Can't you just see them? I wonder if, in an ethereal place, I decided to live a chaste life and that pantomime was placed in front of me so I'd remember. Maybe I'm just terrified. Of passion. Of my passion. And the responsibility of love. Well, once, on my way to the Art Institute, I saw a nun walking on Michigan Avenue. And then, there it went. Whoosh! A big Chicago wind blew her veil right off her head and into Lake Michigan. There it was again! And there I was again. That veil. The one that's over my passion. I want a big Chicago wind to blow my veil away!

Better Places to Go
By David-Matthew Barnes

Judy: late thirties

Seriocomic

> *Judy is lovelorn and a hopeless romantic. Here, she tells a*
> *waitress about her brief love affair with a truck driver who*
> *was passing through the small town that she lives in.*

JUDY: I lay awake at night thinking about him. I know that sounds
crazy, but I can't get that man off of my mind. I hear his voice
while I'm folding the laundry or while I'm making dinner. I stand
at the sink, washing dishes and all I can think about is the touch
of his hand on the back of my neck. I've cracked three glasses
and chipped two plates in only seven days. I'm so turned around,
I can barely remember my own name. I keep my eyes on the
road, waiting for him to appear. Waiting for him to come back
for me and take me away from all of this. I sit in that house, day
after day and night after night and I am surrounded by memo-
ries of my mother. She was a wild woman. She ran off and ended
up in the trunk of a car, covered in gasoline and her mouth
stuffed with dirty rags, choking the life out of her. She was never
a good mother. I don't think she really liked us much. I think we
were always in her way. Like we were a burden. People have
never paid me much attention before. They see right through me.
But he didn't. He liked me and it made me feel something inside.
I'm lonely and I think I've been lonely for a long time. But it was-
n't until I met him that I realized how much the loneliness was
killing me. *(Pauses.)* God, I want to be married, Linda. I want to
have a house of my own with nice wallpaper and *clean* carpet.
(Pauses.) I want children.

Romance
By Barbara Lhota

Miriam: thirties, a medieval literature professor

Seriocomic

> *Miriam, thirties, dances with a mailman, Mick, who she's only just met this late evening in a chapel in Boston around the Christmas season. Tonight, Miriam has left her husband. Mick, the stranger she meets, has just been jilted at the altar at this very chapel. Here Miriam describes the reason her marriage has unraveled.*

MIRIAM: *(She laughs, humming along to "Jingle Bells.")* When we went on our honeymoon, my husband, Morris, told me he had a great Christmas present for me. And I was guessing like a necklace or some real big thing . . . Oh, I can't tell this. I'll be embarrassed. *(She stops dancing.)* Well, he wrapped himself up in Christmas paper, he was nude, and he tied a jingle bell on his . . . well, you know. And it was great. The best — I mean, not the jingle bell. We took it off for safety reasons. *(Beat.)* And now . . . Well, no more bells. *(Pause.)* So I recently . . . I bought this red dress. Perfect. Low-cut but sophisticated. The kind that shows my legs off perfectly. I have nice molded calves, the thighs aren't so fine. *(She models them for him.)* I was so anxious. I waited for him. I felt so, so red in it. So voluptuous. You know? I wanted him so bad. I didn't mean to have him be uncomfortable. I never intended that. This red dress was supposed to cure his problem, OUR problem. So I tried to remain hopeful while he seemed both humiliated and terrified. I knew it was a problem, but we both figured it would go away. But it doesn't. And he blames me. Like I cause it. Like maybe, I don't want him bad enough. Isn't that crazy? And the months go by and it becomes harder to talk about. I thought the dress would . . . I gave it away to a friend. I couldn't look at it. It reminded me of our failure. My failure. I try, I try to get him to talk about it. To go get help. But he shuts down. And I can't take it anymore. I'm so lonely without him. I'm so, so lonely. God, I'm lonely. *(Beat.)* I can't, I can't do this.

Carnality
By Mark Loewenstern

Michelle: twenty-five to thirty-five, focused, perceptive and a little
    manic

Dramatic

*Michelle is explaining to Ben, her ex-husband, why they
can't hug hello and good-bye anymore.*

MICHELLE: Don't take this the wrong way, but it's not like I don't
    meet men who are sexier than you. I do. But you're . . . I don't
    know. You're familiar. I know you. My body knows you. Isn't
    that the word they use in the Bible? Knowing? Adam knew Eve
    and David knew Bathsheba and so on and so on? Well, it's a
    good word for it. Because when you hug me, or touch me, or
    even when we're just alone in a room, I'll think, "This is the man
    I remember. This is the one I used to fall asleep next to." And it
    hardly even matters that at the same time I'll be thinking, "This
    is also the one who drives me up a tree." So, it sucks, Ben.
    Because I don't want you to be the one I feel this way about. I
    want it to be someone I can live with. And I know that someday
    I'm going to find him, but I haven't yet, and it's been a while. It's
    been too long. And I just don't trust myself around you any-
    more. It feels too good when you hold me.

The Space Between Heartbeats
By Kathleen Warnock

Allison: thirties and up, college professor

Dramatic

> *Allison has hired Mandy to help her move to her new apartment. As they are carrying things, Allison's bad shoulder goes out. She's in physical pain at the start of the monologue, but she gradually relaxes as she tells her story. Mandy, who used to be a massage therapist, works on the spasm. Mandy is a lesbian; Allison is slightly uncomfortable with that. She tries to deny the attraction she is beginning to feel for Mandy, and to rationalize why she has always felt closer to women than men.*

ALLISON: I don't . . . I'm not . . . I like guys . . . But, you know, I love my women friends. In some ways there's an emotional intimacy there that . . . well, it just doesn't exist . . . well, not very often . . . between men and women. *(Pause.)* In general, I prefer the company of women. Except to sleep with, of course. I'm being really . . . something. Phobic. But I do want you to know . . . I have experienced real closeness with my women friends . . . some of the most satisfying moments of my life. My roommate in college. Andrea. So talented. A piano performance major . . . strong hands. Like yours. I was still playing violin . . . enough to make my shoulder hurt all the time. And some nights, I'd roll over and just GROAN, and Andrea would get up, and massage my shoulder. She'd rub my arm until I relaxed . . . and it felt so good, that sometimes I'd fall asleep against her. One morning, I woke up, and my head was in her lap, and she was stroking my hair, and looking at me, with the sweetest smile.

It was. A moment. A great one. One of the few moments of pure pleasure I've ever had.

Baby Talk
By Jeanne Dorsey

Sherri: thirties, middle/upper-middle class, high-strung, urban mother/
wife

Seriocomic

> *While her son Dashiell is off playing on the monkey bars,*
> *Sherri sits on a park bench with her friend Helena and with*
> *Kristin, a stranger and adoptive mother with whom the*
> *two friends have been chatting. The three women discuss*
> *motherhood and Sherri blurts out her profound frustrations.*

SHERRI: I never fantasized about being a mother. Mine were fears not
fantasies. Really. I'm sorry. It's just — wow — I get — you know —
it's all so nerve-wracking to me. The whole thing, frankly, the
whole kid-parent-mother-father-husband-wife-lover thing it's a
total fucking house of cards is what it is. I don't know how anybody does it. I don't, I really don't. I can barely cope. That's how
I feel, like most of the time I'm on the verge of collapse. I don't
know how anybody copes with any of it yet everyone does.
Somehow. Like Kristin here, with no partner, but she wants a
child, she travels, she journeys to Ecuador and gets one, raises
him on her own, he's totally adorable and gives her no problem
and everything seems hunky-dory. Me? I'm married to Howard
whom I never see because he works endless hours but we did
manage to conceive the *one* time that we did actually have sex
and now here I am with Dashiell who makes me jump through
hoops and gives me a run for my money and really, what's in it
for me? Company? He does, he keeps me company I'll give him
that. And we have fun, we do, we play huckle buckle beanstalk
or whatever the hell it's called and we laugh really hard and we
hug and he hangs on to my neck for dear life and that's really
sweet but it makes me feel guilty because little does he know that
this lifeboat has a leak. I mean, truthfully, having him wasn't my
fantasy. My real fantasy was having constant sex, that was my
real fantasy and it never came true, even when I got married I
thought for sure we'd have sex all the time and like, guess what?!

Erin Go Bragh-less
By John Shea

Kelly: thirty, Barry's wife, who knows no other way of living. Her subservience to her husband has rendered her helpless, and her dreams of finding a life outside of her home will never be realized. Kelly is fast becoming bitter and depressed, feelings she hides through sarcasm and gossip, pointing the finger at what she considers the faults of others, trying desperately to paint a rosy picture of domestic bliss to cover the dependence on drugs and alcohol that masks the banality and finality of her current position.

Dramatic

After a drunken, violent fight with her husband the night before, Kelly confides in her best friend that she has no choice but to take her husband back, trying to convince herself as well as her friend that the choice she is making is the right one.

KELLY: *(Speaking, concentrating on the burning end of her cigarette, avoiding looking directly at Lisa.)* At least you got to do what you wanted. Me, I got stuck. Am stuck. Look at me. I don't even want to go and pick up my kids. I don't want to see them. Sometimes I don't even like them, don't want to be in the same room with them. Every day they're there to remind me how miserable I am. I thought I was all set. Twenty years old, havin' a baby, gettin' married. What the fuck did I know, that's what I thought I was supposed to do. Nobody ever told me there might be somethin' else. Next thing you know, I'm thirty, have three kids and hate my life. I look at you and think how lucky you are. You can do whatever you want, go anywhere, live your own life. I feel like a prisoner. And what can I do about it? Where am I gonna go with three kids? Who am I kiddin'? I can't get a job. I just tell myself that to make it all seem bearable. I'm stayin' right where I am. Who's gonna hire me with no experience? All I've ever done was have babies and do housework. Big fuckin' skills. Can you imagine what they'd say if I left Barry now? Oh the poor thing, she's gonna have to go on welfare, maybe move back to the projects. They'd love that. This might be it, but it's mine. Yes, I'll take him back. I have to. That time with Steve? It meant nothin'. I just wanted to let Barry know that I knew he was sleepin' around. I never told myself that Steve was gonna leave Maura. I knew I wasn't leavin' Barry, not really, and I certainly wasn't gonna give up my kids for Steve. But for a few short days, I felt free. I knew I'd be back, deep down, I knew. What would I do if I really left? Find someone else to tell me what to do? Barry might not be the best, but at least I know what to expect. That has to count for somethin', doesn't it? *(Light fades on Kelly and Lisa.)*

Heaven and Home
By Matthew A. Everett

Gabby: late twenties to early thirties, bartender

Seriocomic

> *Gabby is speaking to her good friend Cian. Cian is also the younger brother of Vince, Gabby's long-term boyfriend. Vince at times is emotionally distant, never more so than when reminded of Gabby's firm faith in God, particularly in the wake of the untimely death of a close mutual friend. Cian has just asked Gabby if Vince has ever actually said the words, "I love you."*

GABBY: It's just — words. "I love you." Three words. They don't mean anything anymore. No one believes them anymore. I'm not even sure I'd believe them if Vince *did* say them. I probably wouldn't. It's funny, but it's easier to believe God loves me. Because I can't see Him. He's not standing right in front of me. He's not sitting across the kitchen table waiting for His newspaper, wondering why I'm out of milk, waiting for me to leave for church so He can play basketball and not feel guilty. It's easy to believe God loves me. He doesn't have to say it. Someone else tells me and I take it on faith. I read it. I don't have to face Him. Look in His eyes and wonder.

I don't mean that things with Vince are all bad. They're not. He may not say it, but there are so many things he *does*. Good things. He'll stay up all night just talking, holding me in bed. I can't remember the last person I felt comfortable enough to talk with in bed. Laugh with in bed. He shows me. I believe he loves me. Even though we both scrupulously avoid saying it.

Is it enough for me? *(Pause.)*

It's more than I've had in a very long time.

And no. It's not enough.

The Test
By Paul Kahn

Kate: thirty-four, somewhat plain-looking

Dramatic

> *Shy Kate and her loud, self-centered mother are having lunch in a fashionable restaurant. Her mother is visiting from out of town and has insisted on a "girls' day out" of shopping, which Kate is hardly in the mood for. She reminds her mother why she isn't — the imminence of her appointment for a cone biopsy, the test that will determine whether or not she has cervical cancer.*

KATE: It's a cone biopsy, Mom. Can't you even say the words? Maybe they are medical and impersonal sounding. But, calling it something else won't change what it is. Or what it could mean.

Maybe *you* can talk yourself into believing that doctors are just alarmists, and this is all just nothing or a way for them to make money. But I have to face the truth. I have to face myself. I'm thirty-four years old, with no career, still just a secretary doing everyone else's shit work. I have no husband. No kids. And now I might never be able to have any!

Let the goddamned waitress wait! I might lose my fertility. I might even lose my life! And you want to order cocktails?

Don't tell me you're trying to cheer me up. I don't want cheering up. I wish for once in your life you'd just listen to me. Stop interrupting and listen. I'm scared, Mom. I'm so, so scared! And I know there's nothing you can do about it. I'm not asking you to *do* anything. You can't fix this. You can't drink it away. You can just be with me. Just please please be with me!

Brave New Tiger
By Diane Lefer

Jen: single woman in her thirties to forties

Seriocomic

> *Jen has had no luck with men, but when she visits a wildlife research park, as soon as she lays eyes on the Siberian tiger, she's smitten. He is on a long chain but not caged. She walks up to him and, with some trepidation, unchains him. The tiger coughs (which is a friendly tiger greeting), rolls over on his back, and briefly purrs.*

JEN: I didn't expect this to happen — to meet you, to feel this attraction, and this fear. You are gorgeous. Muscle and sinew. Those stripes. And you seem so aware of me, like you're really paying attention. I want to lie down next to you, run my hands through your fur. I forget how dangerous you are, how different.

I haven't had to trust anyone in a long time, but I'm not afraid to be vulnerable. I'm not afraid to take the initiative and tell you exactly how I feel. I can learn to appreciate you as you are and not get my feelings hurt over what you can't give.

You have the biggest, most golden eyes.

I'm not trying to pressure you. But I don't think our differences are, insurmountable.

Except . . . except . . . I need to — I need to pee. Now. Baby . . . Look, I realize, you have instincts. I understand that in your basic cultural worldview, as long as I'm towering over you, we're cool. But as soon as I — I'm going to have to squat. As soon as I'm that low to the ground, I'm prey, right? Only I'm not prey. I'm Jen. Does our relationship have to depend on dominance? On hierarchy? I want us to be equals. Do we have an understanding? Because I really need to . . . go.

From Zero to Sixty in 3.5 Seconds
By Deni Krueger

Jaylene: upper thirties, a sexy woman with the deep, seductive voice of someone who has smoked for many years

Dramatic

Jaylene sits at a table. She is on a blind date and speaks to the man across from her. He has just asked her what she expects from her life.

JAYLENE: I want what every woman wants. *(Jaylene looks at the man across from her and laughs. She takes a long drag, blows it out and watches the smoke. She looks at the cigarette before speaking.)* I know each cigarette takes eleven minutes off my life. I know a first date only ends two ways, together or alone. I know the glorious things a man can do when he touches a woman's body. When he stands so close you can feel his breath behind your ear as he slowly slides his hands from your sides, to your stomach, and then down to the place where you want his fingers most. When he turns you around and leans over to kiss you with lips that barely feel. The hands move faster . . . they grab and squeeze and mold you until you know the secret. And then you give back . . . and you meet with all of your body until you both can't wait anymore. You wrap together, bodies still sliding . . . hand to hand. Moving and pushing against each other until you ache to move faster. So you do. And you move, and rock, and ache . . . and move, and rock, and ache . . . and move, and rock, and ache until you both crash into the stars you see behind your eyes. And then you hold it in your body for as long as it lasts. That's what I want. To be with the love of my life and have all that during my last minutes on earth. But I ain't met a man yet that makes me want that last eleven minutes.

Green-Eyed Monster
By Dennis Schebetta

Suzy: twenties to thirties, a housewife

Comic

> *Suzy and her husband, Frank, have just made love and are*
> *sharing intimate fantasies about who they sometimes think*
> *of when they make love to each other. Suzy has told him*
> *Paul Newman, and Frank reluctantly tells her but only if she*
> *promises not to get jealous.*

SUZY: I'm sorry, what? Miss Piggy?! That's who you think about
when we make love? That's so . . . so . . . bizarre! While the two
of us are locked in a passionate embrace I'm imagining Paul
Newman's gorgeous blue eyes and you're fucking a puppet? And
are you Kermit the Frog in this fantasy? No, I said I wouldn't get
jealous! Of course, I'm upset! Do you have a fondness for Porky
Pig, too? So, what is this, a pig fetish or a puppet thing? Or is it
the oddity of the idea that gets you off. Am I not kinky enough
for you, Frank? If there's something you want me to do in bed,
you just have to tell me. We never do anything exciting. Day
after day it's the same old thing. So, maybe this is a message to
do something crazy. Let's work this kinky-ness out of your system. You and me. Right now. Let's go in the kitchen and get
wild. We'll use an egg beater in indescribable ways. Let's have
sex on the kitchen floor smothered in strawberry jam! No, we'll
get too sticky. Butter! Smothered in butter! Let's make love in a
way no one has ever imagined before. You want dirty? I'll do it.
You want bizarre? I can do bizarre. Please, Frank. I want to be
your Miss Piggy. C'mon, I'll grab the butter.

Mutual Mastication
By Justin Warner

Sharon: thirties, a wholesome-looking but sultry parishioner

Comic

> *Sharon, a new parishioner in a Catholic Church, has been called to Father Kobak's office to discuss her annoying habit of chewing and sucking on her Communion host too loudly. During the meeting, Sharon reveals that she gets a sensual pleasure out of savoring communion wafers that most people would never dream of. Horrified but strangely intrigued, Father Kobak can't help being curious. Here, Sharon tempts him to try enjoying Communion the way she does — and calls his bluff on his true motives for their meeting.*

SHARON: I've seen the way you look at me from the altar, Father. You start long before Communion.

[KOBAK: *I don't know what you're talking about.*]

SHARON: Sometimes I sit on the left side, sometimes on the right. No matter where I am, you're looking at me the whole time.

[KOBAK: *(Cracking.) It's the noise. I just can't deal with . . . the noise . . .*]

SHARON: *(Intently.)* Tell the truth, Father Kobak. If you really can't stand the noise — if listening to me chew the host bothers you *so* much — then why do you always give me such a big piece?

[KOBAK: *Sharon, stop.*]

SHARON: *(She puts her fingers to his lips.)* Shhh. *(Pause. Kobak's resistance is crumbling.)* You know what I learned when I learned how to really enjoy Communion, Father? How to savor it like a fine ripe wine? Patience. If you're calm, and you're patient, wonderful, unexpected things will happen. *(She quietly smacks her lips, relishing the last bit of her host like ambrosia.)*
   There's a little bit of juice left in this one. The end is the best part. Don't you want to find out what it's like? Don't you just want a little taste?

Hot Tub Haggle
By Werner Trieschmann

Coach K: mid-thirties

Comic

Coach K tries to put the moves on a male neighbor selling a hot tub.

COACH K: Yeah. Got a tense trapezius from practice. *(She flexes her shoulders.)* The shoulder. Right there. Ouchee. The damn girls were playing like . . . girls and I had to scream at them. I never like to do that 'cause they're my babies, all awkward floppy arms and legs and acne. We got a strong bond. They love ol' Coach K, even when I make 'em strip down to bras and panties and do a full practice. Sometimes they can barely walk upright, but they'll fight like pent-up wildcats on the floor. Work up a big sweat. Yeah, that's why we need this tub, so I can put 'em in it. Watch 'em in there. A reward for them. And me. How long it take you to fill that there hot tub, Peppy? An hour. I can wait. Maybe we can figure out something else to do. Yeah. Play a little one on one. You and me, Peppy.

Phoebe Makes the News
By Terri Campion

Sandy: an attractive, spunky thirty-four-year-old hostess for a three-star restaurant

Comic

Sandy gives sound advice on love to her new friend Francine, who is waiting to meet her blind date.

SANDY: I would hear his voice. *(Beat.)* No! I wouldn't even have to hear his voice for real. I could just think about hearing his voice or even just picture him in the voice. *(Beat.)* No! Worse that that! I would picture myself in a place where we would meet, like a coffee bar or a park . . . No. No. It got even more abstract than that. I would just visualize myself on my way to meet him at the coffee bar or park and then . . . it would all start! The blood! It rushes up from my toes like it's on a mission! My heart: BOOM BA BOOM BA BOOM!! Until it feels like it's in my trachea and I'm gonna throw it up. And my face! This is not a poker face. I turn beet red. Not attractive. But the worst part is my stomach! It starts crunching and grinding like I've got a Cuisinart on frappe down there. So, I said to myself: This is no way to live. You gotta get it together. What you gotta do, to regain your functioning in this world as a complete human being is . . . demand a little R.E.S.P.E.C.T. That's what you gotta do Francine. And I'm gonna tell you something else and don't you ever forget it: No guy, no matter how rich or how hot, is worth popping a blood vessel over.

Stages
By Jennifer Kirkeby

Susan: a thirty-two-year-old woman. She loves to gossip and stir things up. She is a fast talker, and doesn't usually wait for answers to her questions.

Comic

Susan has rushed to a restaurant to meet her girlfriend, Trish. Susan discovers that Trish has been having an affair with a mime who works at children's parties. At first Susan is horrified and tries to talk some sense into Trish. But when the man in question walks into the restaurant, Susan decides an affair with a mime might not be such a bad idea after all.

SUSAN: So what's the emergency Trish? Did you lose your job? Is Doug leaving you? Oh my God, it isn't cancer is it? What are you smiling about? You're blushing! Oooh! You're having an affair! I knew it! How fabulous! With who? Wait, don't tell me. Dr. Peterson, right? Who could blame you? What a body. Just don't beat yourself up about it. People have affairs every day. *(Beat.)* Who then? *(Beat.)* Milton . . . the mime? Oh, that's rich! That is really rich! That geek that performed at Annie's birthday party? You're kidding, right? You're not kidding. Trish, nobody likes a mime. As a matter of fact, they are hated second only to cellulite. You are just going through an early midlife crisis. Listen to me carefully. There is nothing sexy about a man who wears tights, white face and pretends to be locked in a box. Good lord, Trish. Snap out of it. You're just creatively frustrated . . . or something. Oooh! Look who just walked in. Now *there* is a man. Look at those muscles. That is someone to have an affair with. Trish, he's looking at you! Oh my God, he's coming over here! Act casual. *(To the man.)* Hello. I'm Susan and this is my girlfriend, Trish. Oh, I guess you know her. Well, aren't you going to introduce us, Trish? *(Beat.)* Milton? Milton . . . the mime? Really? I saw you at Annie's birthday party! You were just marvelous! I've never been able to figure out how you guys do that invisible box thing. Fascinating, just fascinating. Well, I'd better go on home. So nice to meet you, Milton. Oh, by the way, do you have a business card?

Herbert and Marian in the Attic
By Matthew J. Hanson

Marian: mid-thirties, an awkward librarian who cannot tell a lie

Comic

Marian discovered Herbert rummaging through the attic of her newly purchased house. It turns out the house used to belong to Herbert's grandmother. After some initial confrontations, the two warm up to each other. Finally as Herbert is about to leave, Marian musters up the courage to ask Herbert out.

MARIAN: Hey Herbert. This reading that I'm going to, it's not the sort of thing that people normally invite their friends to . . . I mean the readers invite their friends, or enemies even, or really they invite just about anybody, but people who are going to see it don't invite other people, but I thought since you like books, and since you like talking to me, and since I like talking to you, and since I'd like to get to know you better and I think you're incredibly attractive . . . If you'd like to get to know me better, and you'd like to come to the reading, that would be nice. Or if you'd like to get to know me better, but don't want to go to the reading I'm sure we could work out something else. I make this really good pasta dish, by which I mean Kraft Macaroni and Cheese. Or we could eat out. At say . . . a restaurant, for example. Also, when I get nervous I just keep talking until somebody interrupts me, so if you'd please jump in I would greatly appreciate it, because I'm really running out of things to say.

Imagine the Love
from *Everyman*
By Elena Kaufman

Ariella: twenty-five to thirty; romantic and quirky, edging on insane

Comic

Ariella is speaking to her imaginary lover while cheating on her imaginary husband.

ARIELLA: *(Breathless.)* I can only stay . . . a few minutes . . . this time. But next week, oh, next week I have a full hour! How lucky we are! The last time you held my face in your hands I had blue fingerprints on my cheeks. All week. Wrap your arms around me, all the way around, squeeze all the air out, like that. Oh, like that, oh yes, a little lower. Ouch, watch my ribs. That hurt, silly. Let me taste your tongue. Give me your tongue! Oh yes, like that. Put your knee up, higher, higher. Tickle my back, like that, oh yes, right there, right in that spot. *(Pleasurable sigh. Man isn't actually doing anything to her.)* Oh, that's luscious. I'll do anything, *anything. (Whispers.)* You want me to? . . . To . . . what? You dirty rascal. You . . . DIRTY . . . RASCAL *(She runs in circles around him.)* I *will* do it. Oh believe me I will, you! *(She casually drops a flower then looks down at it, picks it up.)* What's this? A pink amaryllis, for me? But how did you know it's my favorite? *(Smells it.)* Mmm . . . the scent of first love, the sweet virginal delicate scent of tentative lovely love. How could you have possibly known, we hardly know each other. Ooh, what a lucky girl I am! LUCKY GIRL! *(Stops suddenly and drops to the ground hiding.)* What! Where is he? Did he come already? You know what he'll do to you when he discovers us? *(Giggles, then in singsong voice.)* Do you know what he'll do? He'll tie you up and . . . and he'll . . . he'll torture you! That's all. Shh, I must go now, but wait for me? Oh, *another* kiss? Greedy boy. Just one more, here and here and here. That makes three. Shush now. Good-bye lovely luscious lover. *(Exits waving.)*

Elliot (A Soldier's Fugue)
By Quiara Alegria Hudes

Ginny: twenties to thirties, an army nurse

Dramatic

> *Ginny is a nurse with the Army Nurse Corps. A few days*
> *ago, George arrived at the army hospital with a leg injury*
> *caused by shrapnel during an attack. Ginny has taken care*
> *of his leg, and she has become attracted to George in the*
> *process. In this monologue, Ginny approaches George late*
> *at night, and for the first time reveals her interest in him.*

GINNY: Shh. Don't wake the babies. Can't sleep. Yeah. Nightmares. Weird stuff, I kept seeing your leg. I thought I should check up on you. I was thinking, a private physical therapy session. Clean you up. There's too many bells and whistles in hospitals now. I know how to be a real nurse. You give a dog a bone. Tonight you're going to do like Jesus did. You're going to get up and walk on water. Defy all the odds. And I'm going to do like a circus tamer. Like someone who trains dogs or exotic animals. If you're a good tiger and you do your trick and you don't bite, you get a reward. If you do your dolphin tricks, I give you a fish. Walk to me. See if you can make it. You want a taste of this ripe avocado, you got to pick it off the tree all by yourself.

THE ABUNDANCE by Paul Heller. ©2005 by Paul G. Heller. Reprinted by permission of the author. All inquiries should be addressed to Resilitate@jps.net

ACCEPTANCE LETTER by Barbara Lhota and Janet B. Milstein. ©2003 by Barbara Lhota and Janet B. Milstein. Reprinted by permission of the authors. Originally published in *Forensics Series Volume 2, Duo Practice and Performance: 35 8-10 Minute Original Dramatic Plays.* All inquiries should be directed to Barbara Lhota at blhota@aol.com and to Janet B. Milstein at act4you@msn.com, monologues@msn.com

AIR TRAFFIC by Lauren D. Yee. ©2004 by Lauren D. Yee. Reprinted by permission of the author. All inquiries should be addressed to laurendyee@hotmail.com

ALMOST FULL CIRCLE AT THE GUGGENHEIM by Dianne M. Sposito. ©2004 by Dianne M. Sposito. Reprinted by permission of the author. All inquiries should be addressed to auntdd1@optonline.net

AMONG FRIENDS AND CLUTTER by Lindsay Price. ©1991 by Lindsay Price. Reprinted by permission of the author. All inquiries should be addressed to lindsay@theatrefolk.com

ASIAN INVASION by Lauren D. Yee. ©2004 by Lauren D. Yee. Reprinted by permission of the author. All inquiries should be addressed to laurendyee@hotmail.com

AVENGING GRACE by Terri Campion. ©1995 by Terri Campion. Reprinted by permission of the author. All inquiries should be addressed to tarriecamp@aol.com

AWAY MESSAGE by Kelly DuMar. ©2003 by Kelly DuMar. Reprinted by permission of the author. All inquiries should be addressed to the author at diarydoor@aol.com

THE B SIDE by Katharine Clark Gray. ©2001 by Katharine Clark. Reprinted by permission of the author. All inquiries should be addressed to Katharine Clark Gray, A Chip & A Chair Films, LLC, 1271 Prospect Ave., Fl. 2, Brooklyn, NY 11218; katie@chipchair.com

BABY TALK by Jeanne Dorsey. ©2004 by Jeanne Dorsey. Reprinted by permission of the author. All inquiries should be addressed to dorseyep@earthlink.net

BETHLEHEM, PA by Suzanne Bradbeer. ©2002 by Suzanne Bradbeer. Reprinted by permission of the author. All inquiries should be addressed to suzannebradbeer@aol.com

BETTER PLACES TO GO by David-Matthew Barnes. ©2005 by David-Matthew Barnes. Reprinted by permission of the author. All inquiries should be addressed to info@davidmatthewbarnes.com

BLACK FLAMINGOS by Julius Galacki. ©1995/2004 by Julius Galacki. Reprinted by permission of the author. All inquiries should be addressed to julius.galacki@aya.yale.edu

BOOKENDS by Jonathan Dorf. ©1997 by Jonathan Dorf. Reprinted by

permission of the author. All inquiries should be addressed to reinahardy@yahoo.com; reina@violaproject.org; 4951 N. Oakley, Chicago, IL 60625.

FAST FRIENDS by Adrien Royce. ©1998 by Adrien Royce. Reprinted by permission of the author. All inquiries should be directed to royceadrien@aol.com; VM 212-769-6845.

FEAR AND LOATHING ON THE NILE by Suzanne Bradbeer. ©2002 by Suzanne Bradbeer. Reprinted by permission of the author. All inquiries should be addressed to suzannebradbeer@aol.com

FROM ZERO TO SIXTY IN 3.5 SECONDS by Deni Krueger. ©2004 by Deni Krueger. Reprinted by permission of the author. All inquiries should be addressed to krue22@yahoo.com

GOLDEN GATE by Linda Eisenstein. ©1993 by Linda Eisenstein. Reprinted by permission of the author. All inquiries should be addressed to plays@lindaeisenstein.com; Herone Press, 1378 W. 64 St., Cleveland, OH 44102.

GREEN-EYED MONSTER by Dennis Schebetta. ©2003 by Dennis Schebetta. Reprinted by permission of the author. All inquiries should be addressed to denschebetta@hotmail.com

HEAVEN AND HOME by Matthew A. Everett. ©1996 by Matthew A. Everett. Reprinted by permission of the author. All inquiries should be addressed to mail@matthewaeverett.com, www.matthewaeverett.com

HERBERT AND MARIAN IN THE ATTIC by Matthew J. Hanson. ©2004 by Matthew J. Hanson. Reprinted by permission of the author. All inquiries should be addressed to Matthew J. Hanson, 13277 Valley Creek Trail S., Afton, MN 55001; matthew@matthewjhanson.com

HIGH NOON by Jo J. Adamson. ©2005 by Jo J. Adamson. Reprinted by permission of the author. All inquiries should be addressed to Jowrite00@comcast.net

HOT TUB HAGGLE by Werner Trieschmann. ©2004 by Werner Trieschmann. Reprinted by permission of the author. All inquiries should be addressed to 14415 Huckleberry Drive, Little Rock, Arkansas 72211. E-mail: werner_trieschmann@adg.ardemgaz.com. Web site: wernertplays.com

HUB by Ann Garner. ©2004 by Ann Garner. Reprinted by permission of the author. All inquiries should be addressed to ann@plumlineproductions.com

HUNGOVER FROM THE 80s, book by Adrien Royce, music by Mark Hollmann. ©1992 by Adrien Royce and Mark Hollmann. Reprinted by permission of the authors. All inquiries should be directed to royceadrien@aol.com; VM 212-769-6845.

HURRICANE IRIS by Justin Warner. ©2002 by Justin Warner. Reprinted by permission of the author. All inquiries should be addressed to jwarner@alum.haverford.edu

IF THIS ISN'T LOVE by Jonathan Bernstein. ©2004 by Jonathan Bernstein. Reprinted by permission of the author. All inquiries should be addressed to E-mail: jonnymize@earthlink.net